Tunisia Travel Guide.

Information Tourism

Author
Jesse Russell.

First Printed: 2019.

Publisher:
SONITTEC LTD
College House, 2nd
Floor
17 King Edwards
Road,
Ruislip
London
HA4 7AE

Table of Content

websiteSummary

How Traveling Can Broaden Your Perspective
Tunisia Tourism Information: You may not need a lot of convincing when it comes to finding a reason to travel especially when considering a trip to a foreign country. Exploring the world, seeing new places, and learning about new cultures are just a few of the benefits of traveling. There is value to exploring someplace new and combating the stress of getting out of your comfort zone.

Traveling should be looked at as a journey for personal growth, mental health, and spiritual enlightenment. Taking the time to travel to a new place can both literally and figuratively open your eyes to things you have never seen before. These new experiences allow you to get to know yourself in ways you can't if you stay in the same place.

- ✓ Traveling is wonderful in so many ways:
- ✓ You can indulge your sense of wanderlust.
- ✓ You experience different cultures.
- ✓ Your taste buds get to experience unique foods.
- ✓ You meet all different kinds of people.

As you grow older, your mind evolves and expands to adapt to the new information you receive. Traveling to a new destination is similar in this way, but the learning process occurs at a faster rate. Traveling thrusts you into the unknown and delivers you with a bounty of new information and ideas. The expansion of your mind is one of the greatest benefits of travel. Keep reading to learn six more benefits of traveling.

> Discover Your Purpose: Feeling as though you have a purpose in life is more important than many people realize. A purpose connects you to something bigger than yourself and keeps you moving forward. Your purpose in life can change suddenly and fluidly as you enter new stages in becoming who you are. With each new stage in life, there comes new goals and callings. Traveling can help open your eyes to a new life direction. You may be wandering down a path unaware of where you will end up. Seeing new places and meeting new people can help you break from that path and discover what your true purpose is.

Traveling is an excellent remedy for when you feel you need to refocus on your purpose and goals, or re-evaluate your life path. There is no better time to open your eyes than when your life seems to be out of focus and in need of redirection. You might just be surprised by what you discover and find a new sense of life purpose how traveling changes you.

Traveling is a way to discover parts of yourself that you never knew existed. While traveling, you have no choice but to deal with unexpected situations. For example, how you may typically handle a problem at home might be a completely unacceptable approach when you are in an unfamiliar place without all of the comforts and conveniences of home.

> Be Aware of Your Blessings: When you travel to a new destination, your eyes are opened to new standards, and, you become more aware of all the blessings and privileges you have been given. It is easy to forget what you do have and only focus on what is missing from your life. Traveling can help put things back into perspective and re-center your priorities on what truly matters.

Consider traveling through an area that has no electricity or running water if you come from a place where cold bottled water is easily accessible and nearly anything you want can be delivered to your door in less than an hour. These are two completely different worlds and ways of living. For people who experience a more privileged quality of life, seeing others who live in drastically different situations can help you appreciate what you have and spark an interest for you to lend support to people living elsewhere.

> Find Truth: There's concept, and then there's experience. You can know things from reading them online and listening to a lecture, but to experience something in person is different.

Traveling can help open your eyes to the true kindness and goodness of humanity. There is a myth that when you travel you are on your own, but that simply is not the case. The welcoming attitude and overwhelming hospitality that people give to travelers may be one of the most surprising truths about traveling. Beyond that, you have the whole world to learn about with every place you discover, through every person you meet and every culture you experience.

> Expand Your Mind: A key benefit of traveling, or taking the opportunity to explore on a vacation, is being given the opportunity to expand your mind in ways you can't imagine. If you can allow yourself to travel with an open mind and accept the new experiences and adventures around you, you give your mind the chance to see the world from a new perspective.

Think of it as a spiritual and intellectual enlightenment. You never stop being curious and should always seek out education whenever possible throughout your life. You are doing a disservice to yourself if you choose to close yourself off from the world. It is not always easy to let new ideas in, especially when they are in direct contrast with what you may believe. You have everything you need to grow, you just have to allow yourself to do it.

> Connect to Others: It's easy to forget how similar you are to others, regardless of where you come from, what your background is, or how much money you have. At the end of the day, human beings share more in common with one another than they may choose to admit. When taking a trip to a different country, you may have learned to cast aside what is different and unusual because from the outside, others may not look or act alike. But if you give yourself a chance, you may be surprised to find how minimal and superficial these differences are.

As you notice how you share similar needs, your perspective of your home expands, you become friends with people from different backgrounds and cultures, you realize how everyone is connected. This state of awareness is a jump in consciousness that can help you experience a world-centric view of consciousness more expansive and aware.

> Break Out of Your Shell: Without a doubt, one of the benefits of traveling is that it forces you to step out of your bubble, which can provide you with many emotional health benefits. Yes, it may be uncomfortable and scary to break away from your daily routine, but the rewards are worth it. What you gain in experience and knowledge may outweigh any amount of doubt or apprehension you had before embarking on your journey. Travel also helps you to self-reflect and dig deep into who you are as a person.

Something magical happens when people are put in new situations than they are normally faced with in their everyday life, as behavior becomes more raw and real as a result of being out of your conditioned environment. This not-so-subtle push into the world helps you to become more open and comfortable expressing yourself without the worry of feeling judged.

> See the Big Picture: Life is a limited gift. You must choose to make the most of each day. As you travel and experience more of the world, you may be struck with gratitude and appreciation for all the places you have enjoyed and people you've shared your travels with. You have the power to take control of your life and can inspire you to start doing more.

About Tunisia

Tunisia Introduction

Tunisia, country of North Africa. Tunisia's accessible Mediterranean Sea coastline and strategic location have attracted conquerors and visitors throughout the ages, and its ready access to the Sahara has brought its people into contact with the inhabitants of the African interior.

According to Greek legend, Dido, a princess of Tyre, was the first outsider to settle among the native tribes of what is now Tunisia when she founded the city of Carthage in the 9th century BCE. Although the story is certainly apocryphal, Carthage nonetheless grew into one of the great cities and preeminent powers of antiquity, and its colonies and entrepôts were scattered throughout the western Mediterranean region. Carthage fought a series of wars with its rival, Rome. Rome prevailed in the mid-2nd century BCE, razed Carthage, and ruled the region for the following 500 years. In the 7th century Arab conquerors converted the native Berber (Amazigh) population of North Africa to Islam. The area was ruled by a succession of Islamic dynasties and empires until coming under French colonial rule in the late 19th century. After achieving independence in 1956, Tunisia pursued a progressive social agenda and sought to modernize its economy under two long-serving presidents, Habib Bourguiba and Zine al-Abidine Ben Ali. However, Tunisia remained an authoritarian state with an all-powerful ruling party and no significant institutions of representative government. (For a discussion of political changes in Tunisia in 2011, *see* Jasmine Revolution.)

Tunisia's culture is highly diverse, in part because of long periods of Ottoman and then French rule but also because populations of Jews and Christians have lived among a Muslim majority for centuries. Similarly, the capital, Tunis, blends ancient Arab souks and mosques and modern-style office buildings into one of the most handsome and lively cities in the region. Other cities include Sfax (Ṣafāqis), Sousse (Sūsah), and Gabès (Qābis) on the fertile coast and Kairouan (Al-Qayrawān) and El-Kef (Al-Kāf) in the arid interior.

Tunisia's people are renowned for their conviviality and easygoing approach to daily life, qualities that Albert Memmi captured in his 1955 autobiographical novel *Pillar of Salt*:

The Beauty of the Nation

From broad sweeps of beach overlooked by a tumble of sugar-cube houses, to grand ancient ruins and the vast, rolling dunes of the Sahara, Tunisia encapsulates everything that's enticing about North Africa.

Lose yourself in the maze of medina alleyways inTunis, explore the Maghreban mosques of Kairouan and stand on the shimmering salt flats of Chott El Jerid. Tuck into freshly baked *brik* at a bustling street market, pretend to be a Roman gladiator at El Jem's impressive amphitheatre and hoist yourself onto a camel for a trip into the desert.

Traditionally, sun-seeking tourists came to Tunisia for its beaches lining the Mediterranean, the long, rambling coastline is impressive. There are also tiny coastal villages where fishermen haul in the day's catch on quiet beaches and cobblestone streets are lined with blooming bougainvillea.

But Tunisia is so much more than a seaside destination where visitors lounge on the sands all day long. Join the locals at a café after the last notes of the call to prayer have faded, or puff on apple-scented shisha as you watch old men play dominos. Alternatively, get scrubbed and steamed on a marble slab under the tiled domes of a hammam. Or haggle in the souks, sipping glasses of mint tea while you barter for the best price. Suffice to say the age-old traditions of Tunisian life are still alive and well.

Regarded as one of North Africa's most politically moderate countries, Tunisia balances traditional Islamic culture with modern influences. Beyond the ancient medina, the cities are full of restaurants, cafes and bars, many of which have a European air about them.

Though tourism took a hit in recent years after a number of suicide attacks on tourists and the authority. The Tunisian government is working to improve security in major cities and tourist resorts.

Country guide

Sightseeing

Tunisia sightseeing. Travel guide attractions, sights, nature and touristic places

The best way to get acquainted with culture of Tunisia is to make excursions to its largest cities. In every of them travelers will find various surprises and entertainment. The city of Carthage is well-known as historic centre of the country. Founded in the beginning of the 9th century, Carthage was destroyed and then restored several times. The city reached its peak level of prosperity during the reign of the Roman Empire, so there's no wonder why the most famous landmarks in the city belong to the Roman period the Amphitheater, the Capitol, the Baths of Antoninus and many ancient temples these landmarks are considered the most famous architectural sites of Tunisia. There is also the Lavigerie Museum in Carthage, where visitors will see a grandiose collection of various precious items.

The capital of the country, Tunis, is also home to magnificent architectural places of interest that belong to the 16th 18th centuries: the Grand Mosque, Dar Ben Abdallah and Dar el Bey palaces, and the Mausoleum of Aziza Othmana. The city is famous for its spacious bazaars, where guests can not only buy interesting items and souvenirs, but also see performances of local musicians and dancers. When describing cultural places of attraction in the city, we cannot fail to mention

Bardo Museum that exhibits a rare collection of Roman mosaics. Don't forget to visit the city of Dougga this ancient city has become a major tourist attraction thanks to numerous buildings of the Roman Empire period. Theatre remains the most spectacular landmark of the area. According to calculations of archaeologists, the theatre could sit as many as three thousand viewers. The Mausoleum of Atban and Capitol are located not far away. These buildings were constructed in the 2nd 3rd centuries.

Utica was the first city colonized by the Phoenicians. This happened around the 9th century BC. Nowadays, thousands of travellers arrive to Utica see the ruins of colonial buildings and ancient Phoenician cemeteries. Hammamet is another popular destination rich in entertainment and cultural landmarks. Guests of the city are welcome to attend The International Cultural

Center, several theatres and museums. During a walk on beautiful streets of the city you will see many beautiful mosques on your way, with the Grand Mosque being the oldest one. It was constructed yet in the 13th century. Fans of nature landmarks and eco-friendly rest are recommended to visit the city of Tozeur that is famous for its magnificent parks and interesting museums. The names of local museums sound really original the Museum of 1001 Nights, the Museum of Popular Arts and Traditions (Musée Dar Cheraït) and their exhibitions are no less interesting.

Travelers with kids are recommended to visit the local zoo where they will see exotic birds and animals. Those tourists, who prefer active rest, will find much fun in Tabarka as this city is famous for its large sports centers.

History and Entertainment

The modern country started to be established in the 11th century BC when the Phoenicians formed the city of Carthage. Throughout hundreds of years, it had been one of the largest cities in the northern part of Africa. After the fall of the Phoenicians, it captured many adjacent colonies. In the 3rd century BC, Carthage was one of the biggest countries on the Mediterranean coast. Only the Roman Empire was able to strike it down. In 146, Carthage fell before the Romans who formed a large colony in its territory.

After the division of the Roman Empire in late 5th century, a small kingdom was formed at the site of this colony. Later, it was conquered by Byzantium. An important milestone for the country was the times of the Arab conquest and the Ottoman Empire’s reign. In late 19th century, Tunisia became a French colony. Tunisia gained independence from France and a republic status in 1956.

The most attractive peculiarities of the country are fabulous beaches, multiple thalassotherapy and spa centers, colorful markets with many interesting national products and restaurants where you can taste a lot of unique fish dishes. Local thalassotherapy centers are famous all around the world not accidentally. Special procedures with the use of seawater and muds are carried out here. There are all conditions for you to combine the care for your health and typical recreation at the resort. One of the most popular health resorts is Sousse. There are also the best wellness and spa centers in the country.

On 25 July, local residents annually celebrate an important holiday, the Republic Day. It always goes hand in hand with magnificent national festivities.

On the festive day, there are theatrical and musical performances in the afternoon and fairs and firework shows in the evening. During public holidays, it is very interesting to visit large cities of the country where you can witness especially significant and interesting celebrations.

Tunisia is very popular with shopping enthusiasts. Most of the colorful markets and stores with national products are located in Hammamet. Accessories with natural pearls and corals are very popular with tourists. They are not expensive in local gift shops. Wealthy tourists should certainly pay their attention to hand-made carpets and luxurious clothes of natural silk.

Cities and regions

Djerba Island

Guide to Djerba Island

Sightseeing in Djerba Island what to see. Complete travel guide

Mysterious island of Djerba is the southmost and the hottest sea resort of Tunisia. It's famous to tourists because of its beautiful beaches and luxurious hotels, as well as its excellent thalassotherapy centers and numerous landmarks. Guests of Djerba have a unique opportunity to combine beach leisure with healthcare procedures and walking across historical areas. Djerba is also an excellent choice for active leisure.

Ancient city of Houmt-Souk is the capital of the island. Its symbols are three beautiful mosques: Jemaa Echeikh, Jemaa El Bassi and tukish Jemaa Ettrouk. These buildings in traditional style look really exotic for travelers. The small cream-colored building with balconies and rich blue shutters has really amazing appearance.

Ancient Borj El Kebir fortress is located next to the city. For many years, it has being used to protect island from invaders. It has been built back in 13th century, when Normans have been island's main enemies. Turks were first to conquer this unwinnable fortress in 16th century. It was re-build in Medieval times, but most of fortress original elements survived until this day.

Another important landmark is Borj el-Rous tower situated near the fortress. It has very interesting history: tower was built by the order of Turkish admiral Dragut in celebration of his victory over Spain. The tower was built with the bones of fallen Spanish soldiers. The building survived until 19th century and then was replaced with memorial dedicated to the victims of this bloody battle. Remnants of Spanish soldiers were buried at the nearby Christian cemetery.

Hara El K'bira is one of the oldest buildings of Djerba. According to scientists, it’s about 2,500 years old; it was built in pre-historic time. It's worth mentioning that the synagogue is still working to its purpose.

Massive Djerba Heritage complex is the main cultural object of the island. It's located in the eastern part of Djerba; it houses exciting Lalla Hadria Museum dedicated to Muslim culture. Fifteen spacious halls of the museum retain amazing clay items, traditional clothing, wonderful paintings and lots of interesting wooden crafts. Open air Djerba Explore museum offers its guests an excellent opportunity to visit a traditional local village, take a look inside an unusual building of islanders and explore their daily life. Some of houses feature fully reconstructed interior of the past; there's also pottery at the museum offering national souvenirs.

The most unusual landmark of Djerba is the Crocodile Farm. Over 400 crocodiles, including very rare ones, live there. Tourists who prefer less thrilling adventures are recommended to visit scenic Guellala village. There's an interesting museum dedicated to the one of the most important island craft, pottery.

Djerba is distinguished by a variety of shops and colorful markets. This is a great place to purchase popular Tunis souvenirs and various exclusive items made by local masters. Travelers wishing to buy something exclusive and expensive should take a look at luxurious locally manufactured carpets. All carpets are handmade, and a master can spend several years creating intricate patterns. Shisha, as well as other accessories for smoking, also remains a very popular souvenir.

Adherents of a healthy lifestyle will like handmade leather items. They will be pleased with a variety of handbags, wallets, belts, leather shoes and slippers, and many other items in the national style. Dolls dressed in colorful national costumes are also charming and popular souvenirs. Females simply cannot fail to buy gorgeous silver jewelry with precious and semiprecious stones. Affordable prices in local shops will make it virtually impossible to resist buying something. The town of Guellala is home to historical workshops that make excellent ceramics.

Family trip with kids

Family trip to Djerba Island with children. Ideas on where to go with your child

Every child would find out something new and extraordinarily interesting on Djerba Island. For instance, your children and you can go on a journey on a «pirate ship» with your own privateer crew to the adjacent Flamingo Island. The pirate flotilla leaves at 9am from the Houmt Souk dock. By the way, it's better to buy tickets in advance. However, you can take a chance and just come tight to the dock and try to agree on a good discount. But it's worth trying only if there are still some tickets left. So, you'll have a half-an-hour-sailing and then there will be a stop at the magnificent secluded beach. And you'll actually have an opportunity to see real flamingos. You'll have a couple of hours for water entertainments and then you'll have a lunch (included into the tour price) and then on your way back «pirates» will make you some tea and tell fascinating stories about real Tunisian privateers.

In case if your child tends to always do different activities during a day, then you should go to Djerba Explore Park the local «all in one» kind of park. You can walk around the Djerba Lagoon where your children can see true pink flamingos, take a picture against the old Ras Taguerness Lighthouse, or even simply swim. Concerning the park itself, kids can taste various teas in traditional Tea Rooms, take a look at how locals weaving carpets and colouring ceramics in national colours as well as to learn lots of interesting facts about locals' everyday lives. Moreover, you can also take a walk around a traditional Tunisian village enjoying its narrow streets and small houses.

In addition, children can see a great diversity of the local architecture of different centuries right in the park, too, as well as the interior of original buildings of the past years. What is more, there is the Lalla Hadria Museum there where you together with kids would see household items, pieces of art, and local traditional costumes. And, as children have become satisfied with all those new exciting things they would learn, then it's time for going to crocodile farm (only one of its kind in Tunisia). A crazy amount of crocodiles of many kinds live there. They were brought here from Madagascar, and they've greatly increased their population here by now and presently they just absolutely enjoy their lives. So, if your kids are fond of such animals, then there is an opportunity to try feeding them (the activity takes place in the evenings just about sunsets).

Kids would probably become highly thrilled about the island's culture, in that case, you could have a nice day in Guellala the local centre of pottery. Kids can either just watch how professionals do it or even try themselves to create a plate or a pitcher. Besides, there is the Ethnographic Museum on the hill (with a wonderful view, by the way) where traditional costumes, weapons, tools, and musical instruments of Djerba inhabitants are presented.

You can also visit the Regional Museum near Borj EL Kebir where you'll be told about the most peculiar historical periods of the island. In addition, kids would probably be especially interested in the ancient castle itself. It was built in the 13th century and rebuilt in the 16th one. It looks really severe and its whole look reminds of the times of brave warriors. Kids who are keen on everything unusual would like to go to the ancient El Ghriba Synagogue (more than 2,5 thousand years old).

Houmt Souk the capital is a quite gorgeous eastern city like from cartoons with a number of beautiful mosques. If your children saw Star Wars, then you should visit Ajim. It's not just a traditional local village but the place where there are still original decorations for the world-famous cinematic saga's first episode. Among other things, there is a gentle descent while going deeper into the water, so you can swim there even with babies without any worries.

Furthermore, if your kid is already three-years-old, then he or she can try snorkelling; eight-years-olds can already have diving lessons after which they will get a divers' license and will be allowed to dive in not too deep depths. Above all these, children and you can do such activities as hiking, riding bicycles, night-time fishing in the open sea, water skies, beach football, horse and camel riding on Djerba Island. All in all, you one hundred percent sure won't get bored here.

Culture: sights to visit

Culture of Djerba Island. Places to visit old town, temples, theaters, museums and palaces

One of the most significant attractions of Djerba Island is the El Ghriba Synagogue one of the most ancient in the world and the oldest one in Africa.

According to legend, a girl named Ghriba died here many centuries ago. Her body was set on fire by custom; however, the body didn't burn. Due to this, people believe she was holy so they built the temple in her honour. Yet, there is one more legend: there was a woman who came from a stone that fell down from the skies. She appeared in front of Jews, who came from Jerusalem to Tunisia after Nebuchadnezzar II destroyed the Temple in Jerusalem and told them to build the synagogue right on that place.

One of the first versions of Torah is kept in the El Ghriba (tourists can't take a look at it as it's hidden there). Besides, as the story tells, one of the Talmud's authors is buried also in the synagogue. The building was rebuilt several times (the last one was in 1820). If looking from the outside, it's just unremarkable grey building with a little patio behind the gates which takes you right to the entering doors. The interior of the synagogue is a kind of combination of Muslim traditional sculpted pillars and Jewish white-blue ceramic tiles. What is more, there is a hostel for pilgrims just near the building. Any tourist who would like to see in what conditions Jews who came to the El Ghriba Synagogue live. Entering the synagogue, don't forget to cover your head and to dress decently it's essential for both men and women. Besides, if you decided to come there on your own, a policeman would probably ask you to show your documents.

In case if you're rather fond of Muslim religious constructions, then you definitely should come to Houmt El Souk. The Jemaâ El Ghorba where followers of Maliki come to pray –, the El Sheikh the main mosque of all island's Ibadi –, and the Jemaâ Ettrouk designed in the typical Turkish style are located there.

If you come just a little bit away from the city, you can see the Borj El K'bir Fort which was built in the 13th century. To be more precise, it was constructed in 1284 as a protection of the city from Spanish invaders and pirates. Presently you can find the ruins of that village on the bottom of the ditch. Spaniards conquered the Jemaâ several times, and only in 1560 people managed to subjugate the city in the bloody battle with Turks. The fort was completely reconstructed under the leadership of Ghazi Mustapha. That is the reason why the fort is now often called as Borj El Ghazi Mustapha.

There is an obelisk right in front of the fort which was built in honour of the victory of Turks over Spaniards Borj-el-Riouss. Originally it was a «pyramid» of the defeated Spaniards' heads, not a granite monument. The pyramid had been standing there for almost three centuries from

1560 till1848. After that, locals disassemble the construction and buried the remains of the soldiers at the Christian cemetery. Finally, they established a more civilized monument to the Turks' tactical genius.

Also, Djerba Explore also known as Djerba Heritage is a must see! You can not only a crocodile farm there but a true traditional Tunisian village too. Scientists had scrupulously restored all the buildings including the accurate reproduction of the interior. In addition, a water-collecting camel can be considered as an all-sufficient sight.

Lalla Hadria Museum is also located here. It's dedicated to the mode of life and culture of the local population on the period from the 8th to the 19th centuries. Traditional Tunisian clothes, houseware, pictures, statues, and various stuff made by craftsmen of different times are presented in 15 halls.

As a continuation of your journey in the past, visit Guellala where pottery is highly popular even today. You can see there how people used to create their clay dishes and even try yourself in it.

If you go to the hill not far from the village, you'll stumble upon the Museum of Ethnography. You can find more about local national celebrations, clothing, customs, and traditions of the islanders there. Furthermore, we'd recommend you to visit the museum of local lore which is located near Borj El Kebir. Traditional clothes, wares of precious metals, glass, and ceramics, guns, and tools are presented in the museum.

The Roman road which is mentioned in every guide is today nothing more than a typical freeway that connects the island with the mainland. Anything that would remind us of people who used to live here many and many centuries ago is buried under the asphalt. If you're fond of «Star Wars»m there are still decorations of the films in Ajim village. The city-port of Tatooine where Luke Skywalker met Han Solo and Chewbacca still stands there among the sands.

Attractions & nightlife

City break in Djerba Island. Active leisure ideas for Djerba Island attractions, recreation and nightlife

Those who are keen on leisure activities won't get bored here on the island for sure. For instance, there about a dozen stables all around the territory of the island, so, if you like horse riding, you would have so much fun! There are several routes: short and pretty easy ones (It would take about an hour) and highly complicated (for 2-3 hours) for experienced horsemen. In addition, don't spend too much time on it right on the first day. A horse won't drop you, of course, but your muscles will really heart on the next day for want of practice.

Besides, you can also just spend some time with horses, feed them and even get an individual horseback riding lesson with a professional instructor for a fee. In addition, you can ride the «ships of the deserts» here as well.

If you're rather fond of more dangerous animals than just horses, crocodile farm in Djerba Explore is definitely your choice. This is the only location in Tunis where these reptiles are bred. Even though you won't be allowed to touch an adult Nile crocodile, naturally, you still can watch its habits and how about 40 of these ancient predators are fed. Still, if you extremely want to touch a crocodile anyway, there are also small and much less aggressive species on the farm, so you can even take a picture with them like men other tourists do.

In addition, there is a great variety of tours to a real desert are proposed. For instance, you can go to the Sahara for a day, two (including overnight) or even have a ride on motorbikes, ATVs, or even camels on a settled route.

Both travelers who prefer going on foot and those who would rather ride a bike would surely like the local flat relief without significant changes in elevation. What is more, there are several walking routes which connect the major cities and adjacent villages as well. So, you can easily go hiking for a couple of days. Besides, cyclists would be very glad to hear that traffic here is low and asphalt of quite a high quality. In addition, maximum speed here is just 70 km/h, that is why it’s pretty safe here, and you can even have an intercity journey on your two-wheeled vehicle. Furthermore, car rental is also available.

Water-activities lovers would enjoy staying here too. Wildlife of the local water area is highly rich various fishes, sea stars, rays, and octopuses inhabit it. Also, due to the unusual relief of the bottom and marine life, underwater scenery is exceedingly fascinating.

Lots of ships wrecked here in different periods of time owing a bunch of reasons, like pirate attacks and battles during World War II. Now there are, for example, two Italian warships and a real tank which were sunken in different years.

Or you can also explore the local underwater world just swimming with a mask, as waters here are very calm especially in the mornings. In addition, you can try kitesurfing, surfing, water skies or take sailing yacht steering courses in the capital as well.

The best beaches with perfectly flat sands are located on the north-eastern part of the island. According to the law, a 30-meters-long coastline belongs to the government, so if you go to a public beach, you'll certainly find free loungers, sunshades, and locker rooms. However, on those beaches that belong to hotels, you'll have to pay for all the facilities.

Also, don't miss a chance to try thalassotherapy. But remember to consult your doctor before choosing any particular program. You have to undergo all the procedures during 3-4 days for the full effect.

In case if you're fond of more casual activities, you can play beach volleyball or football or try yourself as a golf player in a local golf club anytime you want. Night-life with its night clubs and bars is concentrated in the capital. There are ones for locals and for tourists there as well. In addition, hookah bars are also located in the city.

Cuisine & restaurants

Cuisine of Djerba Island for gourmets. Places for dinner best restaurants

Having meals here on Djerba Island is as important as, for instance, working or spending time with one's family. Suffice it to say, no self-respecting Tunisian would dare eating standing up or on the move. What is more, the majority of local families wouldn't even warm leftovers from the last dinner but would rather just throw it away and cook a fresh dish. The local cuisine is a kind of mix of Turkish, Spanish, Carthaginian, French, and the island's original cooking traditions. However, it's good to know that there is no one common recipe for each dish; people not just from different families, but even from different towns cook traditional meals in their own way, even that famous harissa.

Concerning restaurants, to make clients feel full is more important than a nice serving, that's why you would be definitely pleasantly surprised by portions size. Remember that most meat and fish hot dishes are considered to be for two, so it might be hard for you to eat a whole meal just on your own. Besides, we would advise you not to order too many appetizers or desserts. The point is that, again, due to the portion size, you likely won't manage to finish up such a great amount of food. In case if you want to grab a bite in a street café, it's better to go the one which is popular among locals. Moreover, it's also better to go to one about which you've heard highly positive recommendations.

As is known, food tends to decay soon in heat. Furthermore, new food can cause digestion issues. Besides, it's a well-known fact that spices are one of the main ingredients in the local cuisine. So, for instance, while you'll desperately looking for something to wash it down, some Tunisian sitting next to you would eat the same dish without batting an eye. That's exactly what is called a «force of habit.» Tips here are not included in a check, so you can just pay it to a waiter separately if you want to (a tip make 10% from an order).

Locals usually start their meal with a roasted red pepper paste, garlic, species, and olive oil. The dish is called «harissa» and there are lots of variations of it it depends on grinding, cooling techniques, and proportions. So, just put some paste on your plate, add oil and then dip a slice of a baguette (which is highly loved by locals). If you're trying it for the first time, don't get too carried away the dish is extremely hot.

Tuna, olive, and salad appetizers are especially good too. And also don't miss to try Omak Houriya salad made from carrots and pumpkins and Mechouia salad with grilled peppers, garlic, and tomatoes. If talking about warm snacks, there are also such ones which can easily be a kind of the main dish as well. One of them is Brik a local kind of patty with potatoes, tuna, eggs, and parsley. A proper Brik must be with a runny yolk and strong flavour of whites.

Tajine an omelette with chicken, potatoes, greens, and onions. The dish is about the size of a whole pie. Other delicious snacks are Kefta meatballs with sauce and grilled seafood. Thick soups with, for instance, cereal and sieved vegetables. Besides, local traditional soups are mostly cooked with a great amount of tomato paste. Shorba with fish or mutton is particularly delicious.

Oh, and don't forget about Couscous a meal made from vegetables, meat, fish or seafood with wheat cereal, pepper, and eggs. People here cook Mesfouf for special occasions a sweat version of Couscous with figs, nuts, and sugar syrup.

As for fish, it's customary to deep-fry, grill, bake it in foil or in salt. You can just choose the one you'd like to have the most. The best time for ordering fish is not-stormy days, as local fishermen will have a really big catch. A finished meal is always cut up and then only filet is served. And, of course, don't forget to squeeze lemon on it!

If you prefer meat, then you can have grilled mutton (ribs and steaks in particular). In case if you're fond of something more exotic, you can taste a lamb head here on the island (its brains and cheeks are the tastiest parts). In restaurants you can order beef as well, but, on the other hand, they serve no pork.

When in Kairouan, buy yourself tremendously tasty cookies with nuts and figs which are called «makhroud». Kaber sweet marzipan balls –, Kaak El Warka a dough ring with or without nut filling –, and Mlyabes little glazed cakes are worth trying as well. Moreover, baklava is highly good too. If you decide to go to a «pâtisserie» pastry-shop, take some sweets made from various kinds of nuts, honey, flour, and powdered sugar.

Concerning beverages, local extremely love very hot green tea with mint, pine nuts or honey. Besides, the drink coffee as well. It can be both «European» café crème or a very strong one with thick coffee ground. If you're looking to try alcohol here, order local wine: Magon, Gris de Tunisie, Muscat de Kelibia.

Traditions & lifestyle

Colors of Djerba Island traditions, festivals, mentality and lifestyle

Planning a trip to Djerba Island, remember that the majority of the local population is Muslim. Islam is the state religion here, so people here pay a church tax along with other ones. Even though Sharia law has no primacy, still it's really important to take islanders' mentality features into account. For instance, you can easily meet a kneeling praying man on the streets. It would be highly inappropriate to stare at a Muslim while he or she is praying, as such occasions are quite common here. In addition, it's also totally improper to look at women in a burqa as well as to take pictures of locals surreptitiously. You can just come and ask a person for permission to take a photo of him or her.

Despite the well-known strict Muslim rules concerning clothes, it's ok to lie topless on the local beaches. However, nudists have to look for a small and remote bay, if they don't want to mess up with police. Wherein, it's better not to walk around the central streets just in shorts and a T-shirt as such a look would actually puzzle local people. As for women, please, refrain from wearing any revealing clothing. Nobody will make you put on a burqa, of course, and most Tunisians would pay attention to the way tourists look like, but, on the other hand, some guys might come to a young woman in a miniskirt and with a plunging neckline approaching to get a room.

In order not to get in trouble with the law, you should abstain from drinking wine, beer, etc. from the bottle right on the streets. Drinking alcohol outside the designated places is forbidden here. Besides, you have to remember that there is the month called Ramadan in the Muslin calendar during which religious observe a strict fast. Though nobody would deny serving you in bars or restaurants in this period, offer locals to have a bite or a drink with is totally rude. The same is about smoking. Moreover, when you're, for instance, in a café, don't look at other people while they're eating under no circumstances.

Sometimes you can see men who are having jasmine sprigs behind one's ear. Sprigs behind the right ear mean that a man is married; behind the left one vice versa. Nevertheless, there is no need for tourists to do the same. Djerba Island is a highly popular tourist destination so don't be surprised if you see "ladies of easy virtue" in the night time it's just because prostitution is legalised in Tunisia.

Be careful with your personal things when going to the overcrowded places as there is a possibility to be robbed by pickpockets. We would advise you to exchange your money in the special department in the hotel you're planning to stay in. However, if there are price tags in a store, then dollars and euros might be accepted as well. But, actually, currency is quite variable here and it's far not always beneficial.

It's not ok to elevate the voice on other people here on the island. Locals are rather calm, poised, and friendly especially to foreigners. But almost nobody speaks English here; you would rather meet those locals who know French. On the other hand, in case if you have some communication problems owing to the language barrier, you can ask policemen to help you, as they especially those who work in the touristic points speak English pretty well and would be glad to help. Here on Djerba Island people always greet each other entering public places (e.g. pubs, shops, restaurants, etc.). And it doesn't even matter what language you speak you'll be understood anyway. Another important fact that you have to keep in your mind is that the conflict between Jews who have been inhabiting the island since the ancient times and Muslims has deteriorated, so conversations about religion are not welcome.

The best time for a journey to Djerba Island is during the huge Ulysse Festival which takes place at the end of July the beginning of August. Diverse concerts and theater performances can be seen on special platforms or just right on the streets. Foreign guests, including various performers from France and the mainland Tunisia, come to the island. One of the most fascinating shows is dance battles. Teams from all over the world participate in it. What is more, people here actively celebrate New Year, Tunisian Independence Day, International Youth Day, Martyrs' Day, International Workers' Day, Tunisia National Day, and International Women's Day too.

Shopping in Djerba Island

Shopping in Djerba Island authentic goods, best outlets, malls and boutiques

Djerba Island is a perfect place for buying diverse authentic souvenirs. If you want to feel the spirit of real trading on Oriental bazaar, then go to the fair. It takes place from 7 a.m. to 1 p.m. on: Mondays in Kairouan, Wednesdays in Ajim, Thursdays in Hannanet, Fridays in Midoun. You can purchase various wares and products by local masters for highly good prices during these periods. And going to any bazaar/market/shop, etc., remember, that if there are no price tags on this or that product, it means that you not just may you should bargain. This process is an essential part of the buying process for traders, so they don't appreciate those people who refuse to bargain. Besides, you are likely to purchase a product for an extremely expensive price if you decide to skip this step. For example, in touristic areas, some traders can sell staff four times more expensive than it actually should cost. Moreover, it's better no to buy souvenirs in shops which are not far from beaches and other overcrowded points. You can just find the same thing but much cheaper in less popular places on the island.

Going shopping, remember that here, just like in all the others Mediterranean countries, almost no stores work in the heat, so it's better not to plan it on the time period from 12 noon till 3 p.m. In addition, local stores also close for holidays and weekends. Concerning Sundays, only large supermarkets are open.

We would also recommend going to an exchange point in a hotel or any large bank in order to get Tunisian dollars instead of your casual ones. In addition, if you exchange a bi sum, don't hesitate to ask for a check. With this check, you'll be able to receive those money you haven't managed to spent back in dollars or euros right in the airport. It's better to save all checks after every buy, actually, in order not to have any troubles at customs.

Try to make some time to have a walk around a medina quarter the «old city». You would find not only regular shops but specialist ones of jewellers, muleskinners, and potters as well.

There is the richest diversity of carpets all over Tunisia in Kairouan. You would definitely find something marvelous for yourself woolen, cashmere, silk items, Berber or nodules ones, of different colours and sizes. It's important to keep in mind that one person can take with only 25 kg of goods out of the country. Carpets are believed to be a national treasure of Tunisia so necessarily ask a seller for a check. Additionally, check if there is a quality certificate on the back coating of a carpet.

Hookahs are sold almost everywhere as they are extremely popular here. If you decide to buy, make sure it's not just a souvenir otherwise, you won't function as it's supposed to.

Painted ceramic products are particularly popular here too. Cups, spoons, bowls of all colours and sized made in the traditional style would be a nice memento. One of the most peculiar things is a «desert rose» a rose-like formation of salt and gypsum crystal clusters that actually remind of a stone flower. The hamsa is an open-hand-shaped amulet which is recognized as protection from fading and evil eye. Various figurine of camels, drums, and pictures or containers with coloured sand. In addition, cashmere products of local production are very popular among tourists too.

Local leatherworkers inherit their secrets from generation to generation for many centuries, so bags, purses, sandals, and backpacks by them are definitely worth buying. Additionally, local jewellery made from gold, silver, and gems is exceptionally attractive as well. However, if you don't want to purchase something rather expensive, you can just buy bijou made in Tunisian style.

Local species would be a very useful «souvenir». Like, harissa one of the most well-known dishes of the island is especially popular among travelers. Olive oil particularly the one with a less than 1% acidity is very tasty. Talking about alcohol drinks, wine from local grapes is actually really nice.

Hammamet

Guide to Hammamet

Sightseeing in Hammamet what to see. Complete travel guide

One of the oldest tourist centers of Tunisia, this city was founded more than five centuries ago. It began attracting travelers actively in the beginning of the 20th century. The city's name is translated as "place for swimming". Indeed, there are so many beaches and secluded coves here. During the archeological excavations here have been uncovered the ruins of ancient villas and swimming pools built by the noble Romans.

Hammamet is considered a fashionable resort. Here you can see music and movie stars, politicians and successful businessmen, who have rest on this resort. However, there are several middle class hotels in the city, so everyone will be able to pick up apartments in accordance with financial resources. First hotels on the coast were built in the 60s; today this part of the resort is considered an old district. Each year new hotels appear in the city. Many of these modern hotels can be classified as luxurious ones. Here you can not only rest in a comfortable environment, but also organize business meetings in conference rooms, or use the service of business centers.

Travelers will be particularly interested in visiting the old part of the city as one of the main attractions is located here. This is Fort Medina that looks like a luxurious oriental palace. The Old Town is the location of beautiful oriental bazaars where you can buy jewelry, beautiful fabrics and souvenirs. You will also see numerous restaurants near the market square. They offer a large selection of national dishes. International Cultural Centre is another remarkable place. This is an open theater that reminds of an ancient Greek arena. Here often take place different musical concerts, theatrical performances and festivals. In addition to this Hammamet is rich in numerous entertainment centers, cinemas and nightclubs. Here everyone is able to pick up an ideal place for rest.

In Hammamet, there is an excellent zoo, the area of which is 36 hectares. It attracts with its beautiful nature. Over 50 animal species dwell in the zoo. The most of them are typical representatives of the African fauna. Zoo visitors can admire lions, cheetahs, crocodiles, and giraffes, and even feed cute lemurs. Almost every day, interesting events take place in the zoo. Its visitors can witness exciting dance and musical performances.

Near the zoo, there is a dolphinarium that is also very popular with tourists. Every day, it holds fiery shows with sea bears and dolphins. The youngest visitors of the dolphinarium have an opportunity to take part in such a show. After the show, the guests can swim with dolphins in the pool and take memorable pictures.

Another interesting attraction is the amusement park called Carthage Land that will certainly impress both children and adults. The park is distinguished not only by a diversity of rides, but also by its beautiful design in the national style. Even the youngest visitors, as well as adult extreme fans, will find here breathtaking rides. As there are a lot of restaurants, cafes and confectioneries, so you will always a place to relax.

Come to Medina to see the most interesting historical attractions. There is the old Beacon Kasba. It protected the coast from pirates in the 9th century. It was destroyed during the battles but was reconstructed again and again. Today, you can have an interesting excursion in the tower. The nearby fortress walls have a fascinating panoramic view of the city.

In the surroundings of Hammamet, there is an old town of Oudna that is famous for its historical attractions too. On its territory, there is an ancient amphitheater and an old aqueduct. Much effort has been recently put into their restoration. The ancient amphitheater is one of the largest theaters in North Africa. Approximately, its initial capacity was almost 16 000 spectators.

Culture: sights to visit

Culture of Hammamet. Places to visit old town, temples, theaters, museums and palaces

Hammamet is considered the most picturesque resort in the country. Its most distinguishing feature is its unique nature. The main historical attraction of the city is the Medina of Hammamet; it is an incredibly beautiful complex of old buildings. The Medina is 300 meters long and 100 meters wide; you can get to it through one of the four gates.

In the center there is the Great Mosque of Medina, the most beautiful and interesting religious attraction of Hammamet. There is also a colorful market here; a walk through it will be a real journey into the past. Within the walls of the Medina there is an interesting Museum of clothing; its collection covers quite a long historical period. A significant part of the Medina is occupied by Kasbah fortress; its history is very interesting. The fortress has repeatedly saved the town from invaders and has witnessed a number of famous historical events.

Close to the Medina there is another important historical site, the tomb of Sidi Bou Hadid. Like many historic buildings, the tomb is fully restored; today it houses a popular restaurant. Among the architectural landmarks of Hammamet, George Sebastian Villa stands out. Built in the early 20th century, it is characterized by an incredibly beautiful style; holidaymakers have an opportunity to stroll through the old mansion and admire its elegant interior. It is decorated with picturesque Roman mirrors, antique furniture and works of art.

Next to it there is the beautiful garden with centuries-old cypress trees. There is also the old pool surrounded by tall pillars and the Roman theater that became the permanent venue for the annual International Festival of Arts. Two ancient cemeteries, French and Islamic, are located to the east of Medina; they are of interest mainly from the architectural point of view.

In the immediate vicinity to Hammamet there is a site, which is sure to interest fans of historic sites. We are talking about the Pupput Roman Site, the predecessor of modern Hammamet. There are numerous religious sites and ancient buildings, each of which has its own unique history.

Attractions & nightlife

City break in Hammamet. Active leisure ideas for Hammamet attractions, recreation and nightlife

Conservative and quiet, Hammamet has gained recognition because of various entertainment options, incredibly beautiful nature and upscale thalassotherapy centers. The city will appeal to those who prefer outdoor activities and would like to spend a lot of time in the fresh air. Those who hope to rest comfortably as a family can also improve their health during holidays.

The biggest beach of the resort is Hammamet Beach. You can rest all the day on the scenic coast enjoying the bright sun and tasting national food in local restaurants. The beach is located in the vicinity of Medina, so it is very popular among visitors.

The resort is equipped with several high-class golf centers; one of the most popular is Citrus. It has an excellent golf school and equipment rental centers; experienced players would like it too. The Yasmine golf center invites to play in calm and relaxed atmosphere; it features a very high quality of service.

Fans of paintball are sure to look into the Zizou Center; it remains one of the most sought-after providers of family entertainment. It has an extensive playground in a very attractive natural surroundings and the most modern equipment.

The picturesque Friguia Park Zoo introduces the diversity of the local fauna; it features a very interesting and beautiful design. There are tigers and leopards, ostriches and meerkats, giraffes and elephants among inhabitants of the zoo. There are also friendly dolphins and seals participating in a spectacular show every single day. There is also a great cafe in a unique national style in the zoo.

The Carthageland amusement park serves visitors every day. In addition to a variety of attractions, it also has a small zoo. Those who come on holiday with small children would enjoy Carthageland. The Sinbad dance bar waits for fans of night entertainment. Shoppers have to pay attention to the large-scale market of Medina; a selection of interesting products in traditional style here is just huge. Popular thalassotherapy centers and spa facilities are usually located in the territory of popular hotels.

Cuisine & restaurants

Cuisine of Hammamet for gourmets. Places for dinner best restaurants

Hammamet would surprise its guests with a variety of dining places; all popular culinary traditions are represented at the resort. The Le Barberousse restaurant is known far outside the city. In addition to popular national food, it serves classic Mediterranean and French cuisine. The restaurant is located in a beautiful historic building near the coastline; it enjoys great popularity among seafood lovers. Specialties of Le Barberousse include shrimp with pineapple, amazing couscous with lamb and tuna; the restaurant also has a fine selection of local wines.

The Canari cafe invites tourists to enjoy branded fruit desserts and ice cream. Visitors are offered to take a table at one of the spacious terraces with panoramic views. There is an extensive menu and reasonable prices among main advantages of Canari.

The Shakespeare restaurant specializes in British cuisine. Spacious and beautifully decorated, it is perfect for banquets. Among the variety of refreshments every visitor will be able to choose the suitable one. Shakespeare presents a decent selection of beer and branded snacks. The beer restaurant is popular among sports fans; every day it shows the most interesting matches on the large TV screen.

Fans of Italian delicacies and those who don't imagine the dinner without classic pasta would be fond of the Da Franco restaurant. Regular visitors say that it serves the best steak in the city and great Italian wines, so the restaurant will certainly please fans of meat delicatessen.

A typical Tunisian cuisine restaurant is La Bella Marina; a selection of local treats here is just huge. Fine seafood and side dishes are the basis of the original restaurant's menu, but there are typical British dishes in it too, including onion soup and steak with rosemary served with a side of fried potatoes. For dessert visitors enjoy tropical fruit or classic English pudding. In the harbor area there is the popular international restaurant Time Out. It is equipped with a picturesque terrace. The restaurant is sure to appeal to fans of simple and hearty food. Fried fish and potato dishes, fresh salads and rice, as well as lots of interesting desserts and drinks are represented in its menu.

Traditions & lifestyle

Colors of Hammamet traditions, festivals, mentality and lifestyle

Cultural features and traditions of local people are largely dictated by religion; the majority of local customs may seem very unusual to foreigners. The French culture has made some interesting adjustments to it, so Hammamet surprises with an original combination of traditional Islamic canons and typical European customs.

Since the middle of the last century, local women have equal rights with men, which is a very unusual fact in Islamic cities. Ladies don't cease to honor canons of Islam; however, that doesn't stop them in getting education and working alongside with men.

Foreign guests can feel relatively calm in Hammamet; urban residents have long been accustomed to a large number of tourists and perceive features of other cultures with understanding. Anyway, you have to consider the outfit carefully, if you hope to visit religious sites and explore suburbs of Hammamet. It is inexcusable to go on a tour around religious sites in low-necked and provocative clothes.

As for locals, they have their own unique clothing style. During a walk through residential areas of the city you can see women dressed in yashmak; many women tend to the obvious European style and prefer to wear trousers and classic blouses in the everyday life. One of the typical national garments are blouses and jackets with Kashmiri patterns, they look very fashionable and elegant. As for men, they do tend to free style of dress;

however, it isn't accepted to appear in public in shorts and T-shirts.

Despite the obvious influence of European culture, ancient beliefs form an integral part of the national way of life. This part of the local culture is manifested in many different areas of life. For example, locals use the hand of Fatima as a talisman. This mascot can be seen in virtually every home and car. Locals use henna to protect themselves from evil. Palms and soles of the feet are decorated with it; women prefer to paint hair with henna. This tradition attracts travelers, but unlike locals, they prefer to do graceful henna tattoos as a memory.

Tips for tourists

Preparing your trip to Hammamet: advices & hints things to do and to obey

1. The local beach is quite calm and has a mild slope to water, so you can relax there even with children. It should be noted that there are no hotels in Hammamet located on the first line. Hotels and coast are divided with the promenade.

2. Going to the beach, don't take valuables without special need. Don't leave clothes and bags unattended; be attentive and monitor your personal belongings in crowded places.

3. Vacationers aren't recommended to buy fruits on the beach, as well as take drinks with ice. Fruits bought in the market or in the store ought to be washed thoroughly. Use only purified bottled water, which is sold in all grocery stores, to drink.

4. You necessarily have to bargain at local markets and in private shops, as it will significantly reduce the price of the item. Bargaining is irrelevant in shopping malls and supermarkets. To make it

easier to pay you need to stock up a sufficient amount of small denomination bills in advance.

5. In restaurants and cafes be sure to leave a tip for good service; it will be greatly appreciated. Tip depends on the place; it is usually 10% of the bill. You can leave a small tip for a maid at the hotel, but it should only be given in hand, as attendants would not dare to take money left in the room.

6. Despite the fact that Hammamet has fairly loose standards of conduct for tourists, you should be attentive to the local culture. Don't walk around historic areas of the city in low-necked and bright clothes; bright dresses and bathing suits are appropriate only on the beach and at the hotel.

7. It is inappropriate to appear on streets in an intoxicated state, as it will be regarded as contempt of the local traditions and a gross violation of public order. Don't eat as you go, as it

is considered a sign of bad manners; this should be done only in designated areas.

8. Fans of photography should be extremely cautious too. You can shoot locals with photo or video camera only with their prior consent; it is prohibited to take pictures of women wearing a yashmak.

9. All local pharmacies have doctors on duty; their services are completely free of charge. You can ask them for the first aid and advice on issues of interest. Blood pressure measuring is free in any pharmacy; if necessary, the doctor can give an injection.

Monastir

Guide to Monastir

Sightseeing in Monastir what to see.
Complete travel guide

One of the most popular resorts in Tunisia, Monastir is a major trading city and training center of the country. The city is famous primarily for its magnificent beaches. They are well equipped for sports, have numerous equipment rental centers and diving schools. You will find many restaurants and cafes that serve fresh seafood on the territory of each beach. La Grotte is known as the most popular fish restaurant; however, if you want to try national Tunisian dishes, Les Sportifs restaurant will be the best choice.

The largest sports center, where you can undergo scuba diving classes, is located near the port. Here you can also participate in the marine ride on a yacht. Golf lovers should definitely visit the new field, which was opened a couple of years ago. There is also a hippodrome for those visitors, who want to try horse riding.

When it comes to describing the historical sights of this place, we suggest attending an excursion to the fortress wall, which is located near the port area. The mausoleum of Bourguiba and an ancient mosque are also located nearby. The Islamic Museum is one of the most popular cultural facilities of Monastir. The museum exhibits a valuable collection of ancient manuscripts that belong to 4 6 centuries. Several halls are devoted to collections of pottery, and the astrolabe made in 927 year is known as one of the most famous exhibits.

The central part of the town is the location of one more significant architectural structure the mausoleum of Bourguiba family. The tomb is decorated with magnificent marble and carved ceramic fragments. In 1980 the mausoleum was decorated with new golden cupolas and two new minarets were also added. The resort is rich in attractions for every taste beach vacation can be mixed with sightseeing, and sport can be followed by fascinating excursions to historical places. Travel to Monastir will bring a lot of unforgettable impressions.

The most significant religious attraction of the city is the Great Mosque. It was built over a thousand years ago. Over the years, the mosque has been repeatedly rebuilt. Now it is a beautiful architectural monument with arches and columns. In the mosque, there is a large courtyard and a spacious hall for prayers, in which it does not get hot even at the height of a hot day. The entrance to the mosque is accessible only to adherents of the Muslim faith, and everyone else is offered to admire the historical monument from the adjacent territory.

The Ribam Fortress located on the coast is the largest and oldest in North Africa. It was built in the 8th century and initially occupied a very small area. With each century, the scale of the defensive structure became more extensive. Now the area of the fortress is more than 4,000 square meters. Many famous warriors are buried on its territory, and several religious shrines are in the fortress. In the fortress, there is a prayer room, next to which is now equipped with a small museum of Islamic art.

A very interesting cultural center is the Museum of Traditional Costume. The main part of its exposition consists of national clothes, which were relevant at the turn of the 19th 20th centuries. In addition to clothing, in the museum there are collections of luxury jewelry, precious stones and products from the finest locally produced silk, which is known for its unique qualities.

One of the favorite vacation spots for Monastir's residents is the picturesque Baladia Park. In addition to landscape decorations and old buildings, in this park one can see a monument to President Habib Bourguibe, convenient walkways and recreation areas with benches around the monument.

On one of the central streets of Monastir, you can see the grand modern building of the Palais des Congrès. Since the construction of this large-scale building with many halls, it is used for a variety of cultural events. Here, exhibitions and meetings with artists are held, and in the center, there is a special stage suitable for performing theatrical productions. Some rooms are only available for business events, but a large part of the halls are accessible to all visitors.

Family trip with kids

Family trip to Monastir with children. Ideas on where to go with your child

Monastir is one of the quietest and picturesque cities of Tunisia. To the whole world, it is famous for its unique historical sites among which is the ancient fortress of Ribat. However, tourists with children will also not be bored here. With the exception of sightseeing of historical attractions, vacationers with kids will be able to diversify leisure time with a lot of attention-grabbing entertainments. There is an excellent modern water park in the city SPONGEBOB which is largely focused on travelers with children. This water park has an extraordinary shallow pool for children with slides and fountains. There is also a swimming pool for grown-ups, surrounded by spacious terraces. The presence of a cafe in the water park makes it possible for visitors to rest here all day long. You can relax in this water park even with young children.

One of the most popular amusement parks in Monastir is Spring Land. This park is quite large. Kids and their parents will have the opportunity to ride along its territory on a colorful locomotive. There are a lot of colorful merry go rounds, playgrounds and attractions in the park. Some attractions will awe even big fans of extreme sports. The territory of the park is decorated with many live trees and ornamental plants, with benches positioned in their shades. During the breaks between excursions to various attractions, guests of the park can look into a café that offers a wide choice of children's favorite treats.

With older children, it is worth visiting the center Karting Monastir. This will be a great place for all the fans of fast driving to unwind. This karting center is outdoors and has trails of various levels of complexity on its terrain. In addition to excellent tracks and modern cars, the park is attractive for its original design. Its territory contains a bunch of colorful sculptures which you can use as background to make spectacular photos. There is also an excellent café in the karting center.

There are not a lot of museums in Monastir. Nonetheless, one of them will be an incredible place for a family visit. This is the Musée du Costume Traditionnel. The exposition of this museum is devoted to the culture and traditions of locals. Among its exhibits are national costumes, interesting handmade ornaments, works of art, and household items. The museum is very small, so children will not get tired of a long excursion. A tour here will bring to your knowledge a lot of interesting information about one of the oldest cities in Tunisia.

Among the most unusual attractions in Monastir, it is worth highlighting the Bateau Pirate. It became a real symbol of the city. This excursion ship is stylized under the real pirate ship. Its team is always dressed in spectacular pirate costumes. On this boat, interesting excursions are conducted along the coast for tourists. It is also a place of interesting entertaining and thematic events. A walk on such a ship will give a lot of emotions to children. Adults will enjoy the sights located on the coast.

Those who simply want to take a walk with children in picturesque places should go to the harbor Monastir Marina. Here you can admire the ships moored by the shore, visit the cafes and restaurants located off the coast, or admire how local fishermen work. The harbor area is well equipped for recreation. You will find many spacious viewing platforms, interesting shops and entertainment centers here. You can rent a boat or a yacht and take the whole family to explore the coastal attractions and the most beautiful concealed beaches.

Sousse

Guide to Sousse

Sightseeing in Sousse what to see. Complete travel guide

This is a famous Mediterranean resort, which is considered an ideal vacation spot for young people. The city is famous for its numerous discotheques, night clubs and bars that can be found almost at every step. In addition to the exciting nightlife, tourists will enjoy picturesque beaches, modern entertainment centers and largest choice of entertainments for everyone.

The local water park located in Port El Kantaoui has quickly become one of the favorite places among visitors. Numerous water slides, pools and breathtaking rides will be genuinely enjoyed by both adults and children. Soula Center is considered the most popular shopping complex of the country. An interesting fact all prices in this shopping center are fixed, so customers do not need to spend much time bargaining with sellers in order to reduce the cost of goods. Caraib Casino is surely one of the most famous nightlife spots of this city. You will also find here an excellent restaurant serving European cuisine. Fans of discos and dance floors simply cannot fail to go to Marokkana and Samara clubs.

House of ice cream is, without a doubt, another very unusual place worth visiting. This is a large cafe that offers more than a hundred of kinds of the popular dessert. Of course, all children will be more than happy to visit such place. Adults may find Brau bar an interesting place as the best beer in the city is served here.

On the territory of Sousse is opened a large botanical garden named Oasis Park El Kantaoui. Here you will find more than 25 000 rare plants, flowers and herbs. You will also find several historical monuments in the city. Great Mosque is obviously is the most striking one. It was built in the 16th century and was partially destroyed in 1943 by the French. Nowadays it is fully restored and the monument continues amazing visitors with its unique architecture and rich decorations of halls. The mosque is located in the central part of Martyr Square, which is also a truly attractive and picturesque place.

The most mysterious attraction is the Sousse catacombs. The total length of underground labyrinths is about 5000 meters. The very first underground tunnels were dug in the 1st 4th centuries AD. Christians from among the local population used them to conduct secret services and to hide in from Roman soldiers. A dry unique climate, typical for this area, has been involved in the perfect keeping of the dungeons. In the city operates a particular museum, where one can see exhibits found in the tombs.

The most popular attraction for nightly visits is El Kantaoui dancing waters. Every night, guests of Sousse can enjoy an enchanting light and music show. A beautiful park is found nearby. You can also visit popular restaurants and cafes. The fountain attracts a huge number of people. It is better to take a place near the fountain in advance to take nice pictures and admire the sight.

Several ancient defensive structures have survived in and around the city. Kasbah fortress is one of them. It was built in the middle of the 9th century. Today, it houses a curious archaeological museum that presents fragments of the oldest mosaics, tombstones, and antique artifacts discovered on the territory of the city and its surroundings. El Zahra park is a real cultural open-air center. There, you'll discover a museum, stylized as a traditional Tunisian village. Every day, they generate activities dedicated to national culture and traditions for their visitors. After dark, is the turn of a laser show. As a result, park visitors can witness wonderful theatrical and musical performances.

Guests of the city are welcome to visit the ancient Ribat fortress, whose construction took place at the turn of the 8th 9th centuries. Once local residents used this fortress to protect themselves from the Berber tribes. Travelers and merchants from the neighboring cities sheltered there. The fortress, whose age is over a thousand years, has been perfectly preserved until today. At present, you can visit some of its beautiful halls and admire the view from the watch tower.

Culture: sights to visit

Culture of Sousse. Places to visit old town, temples, theaters, museums and palaces

One of the most attractive sites for travelers is the old fortress, the walls of which are now housing the Archaeological Museum. Its collection is striking with its diversity; it is one of the most exciting and largest in the country. The museum is divided into several thematic areas. Among its exhibits there are antique statues and tombstones dating back more than a thousand years, mosaics and frescoes, religious attributes and objects of art. The Archaeological Museum is the most visited cultural venue of Sousse and the priority landmark of all sightseeing programs.

The most important religious object is the Grande Mosque built in 851. Recently, a large-scale reconstruction of the mosque took place, due to which the shrine managed to find its original appearance. The majestic building has not only an attractive appearance, but also unique atmosphere of solemnity and peace. A curious object with a long history is the Kasbah of Sousse fortress. According to historical records, it was built in the second half of the 9th century on the site of ancient fortifications. The height of the main tower of the fortress is 30 meters. Its top is equipped with a beautiful viewing platform. It is notable that the main tower of the fortress is still acting as a lighthouse as many hundreds of years ago.

In the western part of the city Sousse Catacombs are situated. They have been found long ago, in 1888. According to scientists, a complex of caves was built no later than the 4th century and served as the pagan necropolis. According to rough estimates, there are not less than 15,000 tombs in the dungeon. During excavation archaeologists have found of a number of unique artifacts in catacombs. After fortification works in the dungeon, the part of catacombs was made available to the public.

Another unusual attraction is the underground cisterns of La Soffra, a monument of the Roman Empire. Their volume is about three thousand cubic meters, which makes the old structure even more unique. Nearby is a miniature Mosquee Bou Ftata occupying area of only 8 square meters. It is believed that this mosque and the Grande Mosque were built by the same architect.

Attractions & nightlife

City break in Sousse. Active leisure ideas for Sousse attractions, recreation and nightlife

In Sousse travelers can enjoy all possible forms of entertainment. Vacationers with children, leisure travelers and fans of bright partying and shopping would find interesting spending time here. Sousse is considered to be one of the most bustling and lively resorts of Tunisia; it is very popular among fans of beach holidays. The most scenic stretch of coast is located in the Port El Kantaoui area. It is suitable for holidays with small children and for sports entertainment; there is a variety of restaurants and bars on the coast for the convenience of tourists.

The guests of Sousse have a great opportunity to combine a beach holiday and a walk around the city with wellness treatments, as the resort is famous for its upscale thalassotherapy centers. They are located mainly in larger resorts. On certain days and hours health centers provide services to all those interested.

Those who can't relax without walking through the beautiful natural places should definitely look into the Oasis Park El Kantaoui Botanical Garden. It has an excellent collection of tropical plants, so a walk through the gardens will give aesthetic pleasure and will certainly be informative. Vacationers with young children will be interested in colorful Aqua Palace water park built for the little ones. The water park features originally designed swimming pools and playgrounds, as well as excellent leisure facilities, so Aqua Palace will appeal not only to children, but also their parents.

For older children the best holiday destination will be the Hannibal Park. After trying numerous rides in action and having lunch in one of the attractive cafes, you can go to the nearby zoo. Its collection of inhabitants is very diverse. Sousse can be called the youth resort, as the choice of discos and nightclubs is just enormous. Saloon, Bananas, Living and Bora-Bora open-air discos conduct theme parties and live entertainment almost every evening.

Those who want to relax in a peaceful ambience are recommended to look into Red Iguana and Bonapart nightclubs. In the heart of the resort Maracana disco is located. Fans of contemporary music can dance there until dawn. Shoppers will enjoy the historic area of the city, as there are souvenir shops and antique shops at every step.

Cuisine & restaurants

Cuisine of Sousse for gourmets. Places for dinner best restaurants

Among many dining places of Sousse each and every guest could choose something special. An interesting restaurant is the Queen. Its menu is a harmonious blend of popular Arabic and French dishes. Queen is one of the most stylish and prestigious restaurants in the city; it often hosts jazz evenings and exciting recreational activities.

The Caracas restaurant is in high demand of travelers; one of the main attractive features of it is affordable price policy. The restaurant's menu includes popular European dishes; you can enjoy burgers and sandwiches, salads and French fries traditional for budget restaurants. Caracas serves excellent pizza too. Its specialty treat is scrambled eggs with chicken. The Dodo restaurant invites visitors to have a break from the bustle of main streets and to try popular dishes. Its visitors can enjoy not only popular Arabic delicacies, but also classic European dishes. The restaurant's menu is updated several times per season.

A typical tourist restaurant is Tip-Top. A full three-course dinner there would cost no more than 20 USD. Delicious couscous, several kinds of pizza and original fish dishes attract hundreds of visitors every day. There is always friendly and relaxed atmosphere in Tip-Top, so this cozy place is perfect for a family holiday. Those who can't imagine a meal without gourmet meats and seafood are recommended to dine in the L'Escargot restaurant. In the evening, there is always a romantic atmosphere in the restaurant. There are many local residents among its regular clients. Restaurant serves visitors until late in the evening. The price policy in L'Escargot is very attractive.

Visitors of the Du People restaurant will be served a cup of mint tea as a welcome drink; while enjoying it, guests can choose their favorite specialties. Cooks are especially good in cooking seafood dishes; a glass of your favorite wine would be offered to complement the meal. The Forum Grill restaurant is located at the picturesque seaside. As you can guess from the name, most skilled chefs there cook dishes on the grill. Regular customers usually enjoy fish treats there.

Traditions & lifestyle

Colors of Sousse traditions, festivals, mentality and lifestyle

Special traditions and customs of local people never cease to amaze foreign visitors with its originality and uniqueness. Every year, thousands of tourists arrive to Sousse from all over the world; for many of them an acquaintance with cultural traditions of citizens becomes the most vibrant and exciting adventure. An integral part of the national culture is the music of Sufis. Melodious musical tunes have changed for hundreds of years; however, they continue to be an important national feature.

A few centuries ago, national songs were sung with accompaniment of Rababa, the one-stringed musical instrument. In those days, folk songs were performed exclusively by women, or rather women's groups that were called Rababia. Today, old musical instruments are replaced with kamandzha, a stringed instrument looking like a violin. The music itself has changed too, retaining only its individuality.

For many travelers the first association with cultural traditions of indigenous people is hammam. A visit to it has long been a tradition not only for locals, but also for tourists. The hammam is often located near the mosque. Modern saunas are multi-purpose sports complexes, as they offer customers high quality massages and beauty treatments. Many interesting traditions are associated with hammam.

For example, men can visit the hammam from dawn until noon, and women have access to the hammam from noon to sunset. Henna has become one of the national features; today it is used for cosmetic purposes in various countries around the world. While in some European countries they use henna mainly for hair care and tattooing, people of Sousse use it a very unusual way.

According to an old tradition, they paint soles of feet with henna. It is believed that this ritual helps to protect you from the evil eye. Residents of Sousse cherish cultural heritage; at the same time, every year a national culture is enriched by new European elements. Those who wish to appreciate traditions and customs of local people are recommended to go to suburbs of Sousse, where national identities are manifested most vividly.

Tips for tourists

Preparing your trip to Sousse: advices & hints things to do and to obey

1. The high tourist season in Sousse is summer. Despite the fact that in summer the temperature doesn't drop below 30 degrees Celsius, the heat is pretty easy to bear and doesn't cause any inconvenience to tourists.

2. You can pay for goods and services with national currency only; the circulation of any other currency is prohibited by law. You can change money at a bank or specialized exchange offices; the exchange rate in all such institutions is about the same.

3. Those, who expect to exchange remaining dinars to another currency after vacations, should definitely keep all receipts issued by banks and exchange offices. Reverse exchange is only possible when suitable currency is available.

4. Travelers who expect to make calls to other cities and countries are recommended to use special street phones. Typically, they are located

close to all major hotels and public institutions, and take coins.

5. It is more convenient to travel around the city by taxi; all cars are painted in bright yellow. Payment is made according to the meter, however, foreign visitors are advised to discuss the cost of services with the driver and to remain vigilant. In the period from 8:00 pm to 7:00 am the tariff for taxis is doubled.

6. Persons over 22 years old can rent a car; a standard set of documents would be necessary. Those who received the driving license less than a year ago may be denied service. In Sousse gasoline is pretty cheap, three liters of fuel will cost about 1 USD.

7. The most popular souvenirs are hand-woven carpets, leather products and ceramics. They are not only of highly artistic performance, but also of

excellent quality. According to customs regulations, export of works of art and historical treasures is possible only if documents are properly executed.

8. For good service it is customary to leave a tip; in restaurants it usually makes up 10% of the total order. Small cash reward is also appropriate to leave for a maid at the hotel, for a guide and tour bus driver.

9. In crowded areas you should closely monitor your personal belongings. Don't take large sums of money and other valuables to the beach; in no case leave bags and pieces of clothing unattended.

Tunis

Guide to Tunis

Sightseeing in Tunis what to see. Complete travel guide

The capital of the country with the same name, this is one of the most popular seaside resorts in the world. The rest here is organized at the highest level beautiful sea, spacious picturesque beaches, mild climate and high level of service wait for tourists from all over the world. All these factors make this resort simply perfect. Besides all these advantages there are numerous historical monuments and iconic places in Tunisia, visitors can always combine unhurried beach rest with interesting and entertaining excursions.

The majority of historic buildings here are also significant religious landmarks. Among the most notable places of interest of the region are the Great Mosque and Habib Bourguiba Mausoleum, which were built in the 10th century. Like the majority of ancient religious buildings, they are distinguished by luxurious design and elegant interior. Here visitors will see beautiful frescoes and mosaics, as well as rich colored marble decoration. Such old places as Dar Ben Abdallah and Dar el-Bey will be no less interesting to tourists. Both buildings were built in the 13th century. The halls of these buildings are decorated with luxurious furniture, and interior courtyards are decorated with antique statues and fountains.

Many art connoisseurs call Bardo Museum the real treasure. This facility is opened at Dar Hussein Palace. The collection of Roman mosaics, which is exhibited in the museum, is the largest one in the world. Doug is the most notable settlement in terms of archeology. Here have been found the ruins of the Capitol and the Forum, which construction lasted in 2 3 centuries. Finally, don't forget to visit El Djem town, which is located not far from Tunis as this is the location of Colosseum. The facility has been kept well, so it is in really good state. This is a landmark of the world level.

In addition to magnificent monuments of the past we simply can't fail to mention beautiful markets of Tunisia. Here you will find all kinds of products, but seafood and sweets remain the leaders among sales, as well as flavorful and unique tea.

Medina is the most popular and most visited area of Tunisia. Many beautiful buildings from different periods in the history of the country have been preserved here. Medina attracts with its colorful street markets. You can purchase jewelry made of silver and natural stones, as well as plenty of popular souvenirs. During the colonial period, several gates have been built in this historic district. They have survived to this day. Bab el Bahr Gate is the most beautiful one. Medina is a great place for hiking. Its best souvenir shops are found on Gemma e Zaytoun Street.

There are several interesting sights on the territory of the New City, including the beautiful Saint Vincent de Paul Cathedral. It is the largest of the remaining buildings of the colonial period. The facade of the cathedral is designed in the best traditions of the Neo-Romanesque style. The cathedral was built at the end of the 19th century by the French. Its interior design has remained almost unchanged.

One of the most beautiful streets of the New City Habib Bourguiba Avenue originates nearby. It is surrounded by slender rows of palm trees and is full of excellent monuments of architecture of the colonial times. It is here that you'll find prestigious hotels. A spectacular Art Nouveau building is occupied by the Hotel du Lac.

For lovers of picturesque corners we can recommend Belvedere Park, one of the most beautiful and largest in the city. Rare species of pine trees, palm, olive, and fig trees grow here. The park is located on the hillside. If you reach its top, you'll enjoy a wonderful panorama of the city. A small zoo operates here, as well as the Museum of Modern Art with a collection of Tunisian artwork.

Not far from the Independence Square, Habib Tamer Garden is found. It pleases with the abundance of greenery and chic design. This garden is decorated in the English style. Beautiful flower gardens and landscape compositions have been formed on its territory. Plenty of fountains support the natural splendor. This place is actually a former old Jewish cemetery. At the beginning of the 20th century, it was agreed to establish a small park here. The park has remained until today.

Useful info

Best transportation means

Travelling through Tunisia roads, airports, railway, bus transportation

The transport infrastructure in Tunisia is quite well developed. The most popular form of public transportation is buses. Depending on the carrier's company, the technical condition of the automobiles also varies. However, every tourist is generally guaranteed a safe and relatively comfortable travel on this type of transport. Also, within the cities, there are particular types of minibuses that stand out among all the others with regards to their color (white with a red horizontal stripe). They are known to commute passengers much faster than regular buses, and their ticket price is also cheaper. It should be noted that in the major cities of Tunisia there is the so-called TGM transport. In fact, it is a regular European tram. The local government regularly allocates money for the purchase of new trams and as a result, moving around the city using this kind of transport is quite comfortable.

The condition of roads in the country is also good, with the best asphalt pavement found in the northern part of the country. Naturally, cars are a fairly common mode of transport among the local population, even though the driving culture in Tunisia is very low and also, every now and again, emergency situations arise on the road. Road signs and markings correspond to international standards. Vehicles used in the country are right-hand driven. Almost the entire territory of Tunisia is accessible by a railway. There are daily train runs between the major cities. Trains do not always meet the high standards of comfort, but most of them are clean and equipped with air conditioning.

In the country also, water transport has received great development. Tourists often choose ferries that transport people from Tunisia to neighboring countries. The advantage of traveling by ferry is that it also provides you with the opportunity to transport your own car or other means of mobility. Also in the coastal areas you will find a variety of cruise ships and yachts, boats and sightseeing boats making regularly runs. The aviation sector has also received considerable development. Within the territory of the country, you will find a local airline called "Tuninter". It specializes in conducting domestic flights. Flight within the country usually does not take more than 60 minutes. In addition, Tunisia has six air harbors, which are designed to receive foreign aircraft.

Main airports and avia transportation

Tunisia is one of the most popular tourist destinations at the height of the beach season, which is why the air transport interchange in the country is at a very high level. In Tunisia, ten airports are currently operating successfully, four of which are international. The main airport of Tunisia is the airport called Tunis-Carthage. This air harbor is situated just a few kilometers from the Country's Capital. Its infrastructure can be described as comfortable and modern. There are comfortable rest compartments, rooms for VIP guests, conference rooms, various shops with colorful souvenirs, as well as Duty Free shops. There are facilities for passengers with children and passengers with disabilities.

The second airport in Tunisia is Enfidha Hammamet. This is a relatively young air Harbor, as it has only been in operations for 6 years. The airport is located on the coastline between Hammamet and Sousse. This is perhaps why it is often chosen by tourists, as from the terminal, it is very convenient to reach the most popular resorts of the country. One thing to note however is that such air harbors as these, are mostly focused on conducting charter flights. The infrastructure is also well developed. The airport is very spacious and provides tourists with everything they need for a comfortable stay. Here you can have a delicious snack, buy souvenirs and gift items, visit the nursery, withdraw money, rent a car, as well as visit shops selling leather goods, European cosmetics and perfumery stores.

Tunisia's next international airport is Habib Bourguiba's air harbor. Not long ago, this airport enjoyed full operations. It however now accepts only foreign charter flights. It is most convenient to fly to this airport if you plan to rest in Monastir, in Mahdia, or in Sousse. The airport of Djerba-Zarzis is considered the most southern of all the international air Harbors of Tunisia. Despite having only a fairly modest infrastructure, all that is necessary for offering passengers a good service has been made available within its territory. There is a small waiting room, decent cafes and bars, a small Duty Free shop, several shops with local products, as well as an ATM, a currency exchange office, and the branch of an international bank.

Railway, bus, water and other transport

The most common form of public transport in Tunisia are buses and trams. There are quite comfortable buses equipped with air-conditioners, shuttling between large cities of the country. Tickets can be purchased at newspaper kiosks or directly from the driver. In addition to one-off tickets, there are reusable tickets that provide you an opportunity to save a lot on transportation. You can also get cheaper tickets that allow you to ride on a minibus and a tram. The quality of the road surface in Tunisia is at a very high level, so it is possible to rent a car if you so desire.

It is worth remembering that the cars in Tunisia are right-hand driven. Gasoline is relatively inexpensive, and petrol stations can be found in even the most remote provinces. Markings and road signs correspond to modern standards, but the driving culture of the local population leaves much to be desired. In order to rent a car, you will need to have an international driver's license, and in some cases also, a credit card. The cost of renting the lowest budget car is about 30 Euros per day. Also, when caught in a desperate situation, travelers can take advantage of hitchhiking, as locals are known to help tourists to travel around the country.

In Tunisia, you can call for a taxi. To move within the same city, you need to book a yellow taxi. If the trip is scheduled to another city however, the so-called “big taxi” is what you would need. The tariff is fixed; calculation with the driver is made according to the taximeter. Another great way to travel in Tunisia, and see the sights, is the railway transport. The network of tracks covers almost the whole country, while also passing near the coast. Both commuter and long-distance trains conduct regular runs.

If there is a need to quickly get from one city to another, you can use any of the local airports. Generally, flights within the country will not take more than an hour. Water transportation, particularly the use of ferries, is yet another means of transportation that enjoys a huge popularity in Tunisia. They travel not only along the coast, but also connect Tunisia with neighboring countries, for example, with France, Italy and others. On the ferry there is an opportunity to transport your own car or bicycle. Cruise ships, yachts and boats now perform not only their usual transportation function, but are also engaged in excursion activities. At the height of the tourist season, the demand with regards to water transport increases.

When to visit climate

Climate and best seasons to visit Tunisia.
Actual weather forecast

Tunisia is dominated by a subtropical climate. The Mediterranean Sea is the main influence on the formation of weather conditions. Summer in the country is very hot and dry. Winter on the contrary, is relatively mild. In the northern part of the country, the subtropical climate is revealed as much as possible within a year. The southern part of the country is situated in a hot tropical zone. Due to the presence of mountains, the northern air masses carrying moisture fall in the form of precipitation in the northern regions of Tunisia.

The coastal zone in the east of Tunisia is characterized by regular cool winds that help to occasionally offer a break from the exhausting heat. Winter in Tunisia is cool; the air temperature in January can drop to as low as 4°C. Throughout the winter, precipitation falls quite often and the strongest seasonal piercing winds blows at the end of February.

With the onset of spring, the weather in the country gradually becomes warm. During the day, the air temperature reaches 15-17°C, and at the end of spring the temperature reaches 27°C. The weather becomes very clear and sunny, although at least 10 rainy days are recorded in April. At the end of May, there may be thunderstorms but immediately after the precipitation, the sun comes out again and the air is filled with heat. With the commencement of summer, the heat in Tunisia becomes stable. During the day, the temperature rarely drops below 30°C. At night, the air temperature can drop by about 12-14°C. There is practically no precipitation in June, and the water temperature is about 20°C. In July, the weather becomes even hotter. During the day, a temperature of 35°C is considered to be normal. The difference between the day and night temperature is not more than 6°C. Water in the sea warms up another 4-5°C and by the end of summer it can reach up to 27°C.

August is considered the hottest month in Tunisia. Sometimes the air can heat up to 50°C. Nevertheless, the air becomes cool and comfortable at night due to the movement of the Mediterranean air masses. Autumn offers a little coolness; the air temperature in September is about 25°C on the average. There are almost no rainy days, but in October there are at least 6 of them already. With the start of November, water in the sea drastically cools down to 17°C. Air temperature is practically almost the same throughout the country; and that is, within 18°C. Nonetheless, the temperature can rise to 26°C in the southern part of the country.

Top periods for vacation in Tunisia

Tunisia is considered a very popular tourist country. First of all, visitors come here to have a wonderful beach holiday. A hot subtropical climate similar to that of the Mediterranean Sea will give everyone a golden tan, likewise presenting the opportunity to enjoy the warm sea. However, it is worth remembering that during the month of August in Tunisia, the temperature often reaches its peak. In recent years, the air within this period can warm up to 50 degrees. Therefore, it is best to go on beach vacation in June, July, and in September, when the country does not have such a debilitating heat. On the other hand, you can relax on the southern coast even at the end of October. The decline in flow of tourists after the beach season is observed from November to April. During this period, the air temperature drops significantly, although this does not prevent many tourists from partaking in sunbathing and enjoying the sea.

In winter, many SPA hotels offer great discounts, so this fad is becoming popular, especially during New Year and Christmas. If the purpose of your vacation is to get acquainted with the cultural and historical heritage of the country, it is best to visit Tunisia in autumn. The weather during this time will no longer be too hot, and it will be possible to stroll through the desert or visit the ruins of Carthage in a comfortable environment. Often, tourists come for diving on the Mediterranean coast. The best time for this is from June, up to the end of September. In August, very spectacular marine festivals and carnivals are held throughout the country. The cruise season in Tunisia lasts from March to October. But then from April to November, fans of yachting come to the country.

Tunisia has a very rich underwater flora and fauna, which is why lovers of fishing often come here. In general, depending on the type of fish you aim to catch, you can go fishing or underwater hunting at any time of the year. However, in the winter time, this activity can be hampered by rain or strong winds. In order to catch sea sponges with the help of a harpoon, it is best to come to Tunisia from June to October. In Tunisia is where you will find the legendary centers of thalassotherapy. It is therefore not a coincidence that tourists quite often come here just for health care. The concept of "tourist season" in this direction of holiday is absent, that is to say, it is an all-year-round affair.

So when panning for such a trip, it is worth noting that it is only the prices for particular resorts that is different from month to month. It is most profitable to come to Tunisia for health improvements during the off-season and in winter. If you want to get acquainted with the local population, it is worth visiting during their national holidays. For instance, the Carthage Festival which takes place in mid-June and the Bedouin Festival held at the end of winter.

Political life

Politics, constitution and administrative structure of Tunisia

Tunisia is a republic whose legislation is based on her Constitution. Adopted in 1959, it is even today still periodically amended and updated. Tunisia is a unitary state with provincial administrative division. In total, there are twenty-three separate provinces in the Country today. At the head of the leadership is the President. It should be noted that his rights in the Republic are quite extensive, which is very unusual for modern republics. The form of government is presidential. The political regime is moderate type authoritarian rule. It is worth noting that the President is not only the Head of State of Tunisia, but he also occupies a leading position in the highest executive body. In addition, the President represents the republic in the international arena, participates in various international negotiations, and defends the interests of his people. He is also the commander-in-chief of the Armed Forces of Tunisia.

According to the Constitution, a person who has already reached the age of forty, but not older than 70 years is eligible to run for the presidency. Elections are done by secret ballot of the local population. It is worth noting that before the adoption of the Constitution in Tunisia, women did not have the right to vote. However, in 1959 the rights of men and women in the political sphere were equaled. The term of office of the President is 5 years. At the same time, according to the legislation, the same individual can hold the office of the President of the country for not more than three terms. Executive power is exercised not only by the President, but also by the government. At the head of the government is the Prime Minister, who is personally appointed by the President. In addition, the President has the right to dismiss the Prime Minister at any time, especially if the parliament requires it. All Ministers of relevant Ministries are also elected by the President of the Country.

Legislative power belongs to the Parliament. It in turn, has a unicameral structure, called the National Assembly. The President has the right to reject any law adopted by Deputies of the

Parliament. The procedure provides for the return of the bill to completion within a two-week period. It is worth noting that the parliament has some control over the government, however, experts refer t it as a formality. To state it more clearly, the Parliament answers only to the President of Tunisia. Election of new deputies is conducted every 5 years. To date, the Parliament has more than 180 members. Only persons who have reached the age of twenty years can participate in the election of deputies to the parliament. At the same time, an obligatory condition is providing proof of being a citizen of Tunisia. In addition, the citizenship status must have been received over a minimum of five years period. With regards to social and economic matters, legislative bodies are assisted by a specially created specialized advisory body.

In accordance with the Constitution, since the gaining of independence by the republic, a multi-party system began to dominate the Tunisian political arena. This helped to create a much stable political climate, thereby reducing the occurrence of serious public unrests. Every year, the opposition lays out its political manifesto and makes a significant contribution towards the discussion and the formation of state policies, including the external one. The opposition parties are the Progressive Democratic Party and the Democratic Forum, which upholds the rights and freedoms of the working population of Tunisia. The "Democratic Constitutional Union Party" has been in power for the past several years. It is worth noting that this political party was not long ago (in last quarter of the century) considered the only legal one in the country, having being able to garner a stable number of followers among the local population. Currently, it is the deputies of this particular party that play the leading role in shaping the political future of the republic.

The Constitution of the Country made provision for an independent court. Each Judge is personally appointed by the President of the Republic. The supreme council of the magistracy is responsible for proposing candidates. The main court in the country is the Supreme Court, followed by a state security court and a military court. There are also other courts in the country such as the appellate courts, central judicial bodies, cassation courts, the General Prosecutor's Office, as well as cantonal courts. The Tunisian Armed Forces has more than 35,000 personnel. The gendarmerie, which has more than 2500 personnel, helps to maintain law and order within the country. Annually, Tunisia spends at least 2% of GDP on security. The main part of the Armed Forces is the land forces. The Air Force and the National Guard are also present.

Economics and GDP

National economy of Tunisia industries, GDP and prosperity level

Before Tunisia became an independent republic, it was considered an agrarian country. However, from 1959, the industrial base in the territory of Tunisia began to develop actively. Experts believe that the overall economic set-up of Tunisia depends directly on the export of oil and various minerals that are found in the country. A major contribution to the economy comes from the material processing sphere, as well as tourism. The state devotes much attention to the agriculture sector, however its profit indicators are much less when compared to revenue gotten from the oil and solid minerals sector. Many note that the economic situation in Tunisia has improved significantly in recent years, thanks to the approval of the necessary reforms for the development of domestic and foreign policy and due to successfully concluded trade relations.

Today in Tunisia, most of the output from oil production is exported, which makes it possible to fully improve the country's foreign reserve. In addition, large foreign exchange earnings also come from the export of the national fruit finik and olive oil. Over the past two decades, Tunisia's industry has been developing at an incredibly high pace. This also contributed to the influx of foreign capital. Such investments consequently made it possible to open up new industrial facilities and provide employment for the majority of the able-bodied population. The main branch of the economy is the mining industry. In addition to energy resources, phosphorite is also produced here. They are also actively exported. Lead and zinc were first mined in Tunisia about a hundred years ago. Despite the fact that the deposits of these ores, as well as other non-ferrous metals, are depleted, extraction activities are still ongoing.

The field of mechanical engineering in Tunisia is also developed at sufficiently high level. For the most part it comprises of car assembly factory that collect trucks and motor cars of famous Italian and French brands. It is necessary to pay attention to the chemical industry as well. In Tunisia, huge volumes of sulfuric and phosphoric acid are produced. They are afterwards exported, thereby bringing a fairly large profit to the country. Agriculture in Tunisia has attracted high capital investment from the state. Land reform carried out several years ago yielded the expected benefits and now the land is used with maximum efficiency.

It is worth noting that in addition to grain crops, there are more than fifty million olive trees being grown in the country. This enables Tunisia to produce large volumes of olive oil. Overall output account for approximately 10% of the total olive oil produced in the world. Vegetable farming in Tunisia has not received much attention, although tomatoes and red pepper are still grown here. Special attention should be paid to tourism. Tunisia not only profitably takes advantage of its territorial location but also the presence within its territory of a huge numbers of natural monuments, as well as historical artifacts, such as the ruins of Carthage. Tunisia's warm climate is known to attract hundreds of thousands of tourists every year. The contribution of tourism to date is measured in several billions of dollars annually.

As for the manufacturing industry, it is dominated by the textile and clothing industries. Much of what is produced is exported. In addition, other products from the manufacturing industry include cement, footwear, various tobacco products, pulp and paper products, as well as furniture products. At present, foreign trade in Tunisia has not become normal yet. According to last year's data, the country still has a deficit, as the cost of imported products is much higher than the profit from products exported. Above all, Tunisia purchases machines and various equipment, as well as refined products, food, wood and lots more.

With regards to exports, the dominant role is played by leather products, products from the chemical industry, transportation equipment, lubricants, fuel, and mineral raw materials. The main trading partners of Tunisia are Germany, France, and Italy. The country's GDP according to the data of last year was about 49 million dollars, and GDP per capita is about 11,000 dollars. More than 55% of the total GDP comes from profit in the service sector. To date, Tunisia has more than 4,000 working-age population, most of whom are employed in the service sector. The unemployment rate as of last year's data is 12%. The percentage of the population living below the poverty line is 4%.

The Land

Tunisia is bounded by Algeria to the west and southwest, by Libya to the southeast, and by the Mediterranean Sea to the east and north.

Relief

Tunisia is characterized by moderate relief. The Tunisian Dorsale, or High Tell, a southwest-northeast–trending mountain range that is an extension of the Saharan Atlas(Atlas Saharien) of Algeria, tapers off in the direction of the Sharīk

(Cape Bon) Peninsula in the northeast, south of the Gulf of Tunis. The highest mountain, Mount Chambi (Al-Shaʿnabī), located near the centre of the Algerian border, rises to 5,066 feet (1,544 metres), while Mount Zaghwān (Zaghouan), about 30 miles (50 km) southwest of Tunis, reaches 4,249 feet (1,295 metres). Between the limestone peaks of the central Tunisian Dorsale and the mountains of the Northern Tell which include the sandstone ridges of the Kroumirie Mountains in the northwest that reach elevations of 3,000 feet (900 metres) and the Mogods, a mountain range running along the deeply indented coastline to the north, lies the Majardah (Medjerda) River valley, formed by a series of ancient lake basins covered with alluvium. This valley was once the granary of ancient Rome and has remained to this day the richest grain-producing region of Tunisia.

To the south of the Tunisian Dorsale lies a hilly region known as the Haute Steppe (High Steppes) in the west and the Basse Steppe (Low Steppes) in the east. These have elevations ranging from about 600 to 1,500 feet (180 to 460 metres) and are crossed by secondary ranges trending north-south. Farther south there is a series of *chott* (or *shaṭṭ*; salty lake) depressions. Large plains border the eastern coasts; south of Sousse lies Al-Sāḥil (Sahel) and south of Gabès is Al-Jifārah (Gefara) Plain. The extreme south is largely sandy desert, much of it part of the Great Eastern Erg of the Sahara.

Drainage

The major drainage feature of the north is the Majardah River, the country's only perennially flowing stream, which cuts the Majardah valley before emptying into the Gulf of Tunis, near the site of ancient Carthage. Farther south, streams are intermittent and largely localized in the form of wadis, which are subject to seasonal flooding and terminate inland in *chotts*. In the country's most southerly regions, within the Sahara, even these seasonal streams are rare. As in other countries of this arid region, access to water is a major concern. During the 1990s the government sponsored the construction of a number of dams to control flooding, preserve runoff, and recharge the water table.

Soils

Tunisia's most fertile soils are found in the well-watered intermontane valleys in the north, where rich sandy clay soils formed from alluvium or soils high in lime content cover the valley bottoms and plains. Aside from these and from the plains of the Haute Steppe region, where some clay soils of medium fertility may be found, soils in the rest of the country tend to be rocky or sandy. In the dry south, moreover, they are often also saline because of excessive evaporation. The humid coastal plain in the east, running between the Gulf of Hammamet and the Gulf of Gabes, where Tunisia's thriving olive plantations are found, is the most agriculturally productive of these coarse-textured soil areas.

Climate

Tunisia is situated in the warm temperate zone between latitudes 37° and 30° N. In the north the climate is Mediterranean, characterized by mild, rainy winters and hot, dry summers with no marked intervening seasons. This changes southward to semiarid conditions on the steppes and to desert in the far south. Saharan influences give rise to the sirocco, a seasonal hot, blasting wind from the south that can have a serious drying effect on vegetation.

Temperatures are moderated by the sea, being less extreme at Sousse on the coast, for example, than at Kairouan (Al-Qayrawān) inland. Temperatures at Sousse average 44 °F (7 °C) in January and 89 °F (32 °C) in August. Comparable temperatures at Kairouan are 40 °F (4 °C) in January and 99 °F (37 °C) in August. Africa's highest temperature, about 131 °F (55 °C), was recorded in Kebili, a town in central Tunisia.

The amount of precipitation, all falling as rain, varies considerably from north to south. A mean annual rainfall of about 60 inches (1,520 mm) occurs in the Kroumirie Mountains in northwestern Tunisia, making it the wettest region in North Africa, as compared with less than 4 inches (100 mm) at Tozeur (Tawzar) in the southwest. Generally, from mid-autumn to mid-spring, when three-fourths of the annual total occurs, northern Tunisia receives more than 16 inches of rainfall, and the steppe region receives from 4 to 16 inches (100 to 400 mm). Amounts are also highly irregular from one year to another, and irregularity increases southward toward the desert. Harvests vary as a result, being poor in dry years.

Plant and animal life

The vegetation and animal life of the country are affected by these erratic climatic conditions. From north to south, the cork oak forest of the Kroumirie Mountains, with its fern undergrowth sheltering wild boars, gives way to scrub and steppes covered with esparto grass and populated with small game and to the desert, where hunting is forbidden so as to preserve the remaining gazelles. Scorpions are found in all regions; among dangerous snakes are the horned viper and the cobra. Desert locusts sometimes damage crops in the southern part of the country. Ichkeul National

Park, in the northernmost part of the country, was named a UNESCO World Heritage site in 1980. It is important as a winter sanctuary for such birds as the greylag goose, coot, and wigeon.

The People

Ethnic groups

The population of Tunisia is essentially Arab Berber. However, throughout the centuries Tunisia has received various waves of immigration that have included Phoenicians, sub-Saharan Africans, Jews, Romans, Vandals, and Arabs; Muslim refugees from Sicily settled in Al-Sāḥil after their homeland was captured by the Normans in 1091. The most notable immigration was that of the Spanish Moors (Muslims), which began after the fall of Sevilla(Seville), Spain, as a result of the Reconquista in 1248 and which turned into a veritable exodus in the early 17th century. As a result, some 200,000 Spanish Muslims settled in the area of Tunis, in the Majardah valley, and on the Sharīk Peninsula in the north, bringing with them their urban culture and more advanced agricultural and irrigation techniques. Finally, from the 16th to the 19th century, the Ottomans brought their own blend of Asian and European traditions. This great ethnic diversity is still seen in the variety of Tunisian family names.

Languages and Religion

From a linguistic point of view, Tunisia is the most homogeneous and integral country of the modern day Maghreb. Almost all the locals can speak the so-called Tunisian dialect which is of Arabic extraction. Among linguists, it is known as Derja. By its linguistic structure, this dialect some sort of derivative of the classical Arabic language. However, in practice, most words in the dialect are structurally and phonetically unlike classical

Arabic. Most likely, this was influenced by the history of the formation of Tunisia as a state and its geographical location. Periodic migration and a change of government within the state also left a mark on the linguistic sphere of Tunisia. To date, you will even find in their dialect borrowed words from French and Italian, German and Spanish, and even some adverbs from Berber.

Despite this, the Arabic language is regarded as the only official language in the territory of Tunisia. All official documentation is compiled with it. Deputies and other public office holders communicate in it. In addition, signboards and advertising information, as well as the menu in restaurants and price lists in shops are written in Arabic. Children, beginning from their first class at school are taught using classical Arabic, which is also actively used in trade relations. Every literate Tunisian speaks excellent classical Arabic. In everyday life however, the local Darius dialect is employed. In view of the development of the tourism business, all the service personnel working in this sector are bona fide polyglots. They can clearly communicate in English, French, German and even Russian.

Not so long ago, by historical standards, there was a French protectorate in Tunisia. The French language at that time was recognized as a state language, while also widespread in all spheres of the national life of the Country. Even though Tunisia has gained independence, the language continues to thrive and develop in the Country. It is still highly regarded and spoken by most of the local population. Even at school, it is studied from the second grade. In some restaurants and cafes in major tourist cities, the menu besides being in Arabic is also written in French. Until now, the authorities of Tunisia did not prohibit the production of printed publications and literature in classical French.

Islam is considered the predominating religious direction in Tunisia. According to the data of last year, almost 95% of the local population consider themselves to be believers; most of them consider themselves to be Muslims. In addition, Judaism and even Christianity are common in the country. The Constitution of Tunisia guarantees freedom and the right to choose one's religion. Any manifestation of intolerance towards a religious faith is punishable. It is worth noting that the religion of Islam as is practiced in Tunisia is quite diverse. The fact is that many Tunisian Muslims are Sunnis, but those who live on the island of Djerba profess a religion based on orthodox Islam.

Religious education in the country is at a very high level. From childhood, children are taught to help one's neighbor, so practically almost every Muslim passing by the poor, seeks to give alms. That aside, thanks to modern Western trends, in the territory of Tunisia there are those who do not want to follow the rules of many generations of their ancestors and wish to simply disregard any religious denominations. It is worth noting that the local population is very demanding regarding the fulfillment of the basic canons of their religion. It is for this reason that tourist while staying in a Muslim country, are recommended to observe some rules adopted in this religious direction. For example, women should not wear revealing outfits. The shoulder or cleavage zones should likewise not be exposed.

Within this sufficiently large and powerful Muslim society that is Tunisia, there are still some ethno-confessional groups. All of them put together however, do not exceed 1% of believers in the country. It is worth noting that such religions do not experience development. Belonging to this category are the Berber-speaking Ibadis, renegade Christians and even the Hanafis, who consider themselves to be the true descendants of the Turks. There is likewise also the Jews who were expelled from Spain 6 centuries ago. Of course, during the Second World War most of them did move to Israel and France, but to date, there are still at least 20,000 Jews in Tunisia. They zealously guard their religion and try to pass it on to every new generation.

Settlement patterns

Tunisia is divided into four natural and demographic regions: the north, which is relatively fertile and well watered; the semiarid central region; Al-Sāḥil in the east-central coastal region, which is preeminently olive-growing country; and the desert south, where, except in the oases, all vegetation disappears. In the central and southern regions, there are still people who have preserved a certain cohesion through following a seminomadic way of life. In the north and east, on the other hand, particularly along the coasts, the population is quite mixed and more dense, the life of the cultivator is more complex, the villages are more crowded, and the cities are larger. City populations have expanded at the expense of the countryside and by the early 21st century had incorporated about two-thirds of the country's people. About one-fifth of Tunisia's population lives in the urban agglomeration of Tunis alone. Growth has also been significant in the cities of Bizerte, Gabès, Sfax, and Sousse.

Demographic trends

The population of Tunisia doubled during the last three decades of the 20th century. The country's natural growth rate is less rapid, however, than those of the other North African countries, a feat accomplished through family planning to lower the birth rate Tunisia has one of the lowest birth rates on the African continent and by raising the social, economic, and legal status of women. Emigration has also helped depress the overall growth rate, with hundreds of thousands of Tunisians being employed abroad, notably in France and in the countries of the Middle East. Tunisia's relatively favourable demographic situation is reflected in its high life expectancy (among the highest in Africa), higher living standards, declining infant mortality rate, marriage at older age, and progressive aging of the population. Slightly less than half of the population is between 15 and 44 years of age. Average life expectancy is about 76 years.

The Economy

Tunisia has a well-diversified economy, although it remains dominated by only a few large sectors. The economy depends heavily on mineral exports, especially petroleum and phosphates, a growing manufacturing sector that has received much investment, and agricultural products. Tourism is also a significant source of revenue and foreign exchange, as are remittances from migrant workers living abroad. While foreign debt has been brought under control, the country continues to suffer from a regional imbalance between the north and Al-Sāḥil region, which are more fertile and more economically developed, and the arid central and southern regions, which have fewer natural advantages.

After a brief experiment with socialism in the 1960s, Tunisia shifted its economic doctrine toward a mixed planned and market economy. However, the economy fell into crisis in the early

1980s, the result of an overreliance on oil revenues, foreign aid, and labour remittances. In the mid-1980s a comprehensive program was introduced to liberalize the economy, which helped restore Tunisia's international credit standing, stabilize public finances, reduce budget deficits and inflation, improve trade balances, and increase foreign and domestic investments. Public-sector reforms, deregulation, and privatization have also been implemented. The program has not been without its social costs, however, as unemployment and poverty levels rose. Nonetheless, the country's per capita gross national product has continued to grow steadily.

Agriculture, forestry, and fishing

Some two-thirds of Tunisia is suitable for farming, and about one-fifth of the working population is employed in agriculture, yet agricultural production is still insufficient to meet the needs of

Tunisia's growing population and contributes only about one-twelfth of gross domestic product (GDP). Cereals, in particular, must be imported, as must meat and dairy products; sheep, goats, and cattle are raised but not in numbers sufficient to supply domestic demand. The low crop yields are in part caused by the division of the property into small, inefficient plots and also by the predominance of outdated farming methods. Climatic variations periodic droughts and sporadic rainfall often jeopardize harvests. Much of the country's most recent agricultural investment since the late 20th century has focused on irrigation schemes, well and dam construction, and programs to prevent soil erosion and desertification. Reforms have also freed up agricultural prices by removing artificial price supports. Tunisia nonetheless exports a fair amount of agricultural produce. The principal commodities are citrus fruits, olive oil, grapes, tomatoes, melons, figs, and dates.

The lumber sector is essentially confined to exploiting oak and cork from the Kroumirie Mountains of the north, while the esparto grass of the plains is used to manufacture quality paper. The expanding fishing industry, centred on the eastern port city of Sfax, also contributes to the country's exports. Primary catches include sardines, mackerels, and cuttlefish.

Resources and power

Tunisia's natural resources are relatively meagre. Until the discovery of petroleum, the principal mineral resource was phosphate; of this, one-third is exported, and the remainder is used by domestic chemical industries. Fertilizer is also an important export. Other major mineral resources are zinc, lead, barite, and iron.

Petroleum was discovered in the extreme south in 1964 at Al-Burmah (El-Borma) field. Although Tunisia's deposits are much smaller than those of its larger neighbours, they are significant to the economy. As production fell in the 1980s, the government began developing several of the country's smaller oil fields. Nearly a dozen deposits were being exploited by the early 1990s, the largest fields being Al-Burmah and Al-Dūlāb in southern Tunisia near the Algerian border, Sīdī al-Yatāʾim (Sidi el-Itayem) north of Sfax, the Ashtart field in the Gulf of Gabes, and the Tazarka (Tāzirkah) field in the Gulf of Hammamet.

In the early 1990s Tunisia's petroleum reserves were estimated to be sufficient to maintain the country's low rate of extraction for several decades but insufficient to prevent Tunisia because of increased domestic consumption and inadequate refinement facilities from becoming a net importer of petroleum products. Since then, natural gas production has been significantly increased, and foreign investment has been encouraged in the sector. Major British investments in Al-Miskar field in the mid-1990s contributed to Tunisia's achieving self-sufficiency in natural gas production. Like petroleum and despite new discoveries, the quantities of natural gas are small as compared with Libyan and Algerian production. In addition, Tunisia receives royalties on the gas that is pumped through a pipeline running through Tunisia, connecting the Algerian gas fields to Sicily.

Most electricity is generated by thermal means, including newer plants fired by natural gas and fuel oil. Some solar power is also being utilized.

Manufacturing

Manufacturing contributes roughly one-sixth of GDP and employs an equal proportion of the population. The development of manufacturing in Tunisia has historically encountered two major difficulties: raw material and power supplies are inadequate, and the domestic market is limited. Since independence was achieved in 1956, some notable and sometimes costly projects, such as the Menzel Bourguiba (Manzil Bū Ruqaybah) iron-smelting complex located near Bizerte, have been successfully established. In general, however, the manufacturing base has remained relatively small and overly concentrated on making clothes, textiles, leather goods, and food products. Tunisia's industry became increasingly export-oriented during the 1970s, but it remained uncompetitive and overprotected and did not generate sufficient income. It also continued to be largely concentrated in wealthier coastal areas, despite government incentives to relocate to the country's western and southern parts.

As a result of reforms, Tunisian manufacturing has become much more diversified, with new investments in the production and export of mechanical and electromechanical equipment, petroleum products, and chemicals. The textile sector still remains disproportionately large, however, and more than one-third of all manufacturing operations are located in Tunis alone. On the other hand, investment codes introduced in the late 1980s have attracted strong foreign interest, which has enhanced technology transfer, modernized the service and financial sectors, and aided export development.

Privatization has been a slower process. After an initial flurry of sales in the early 1990s, the pace slackened, and privatization seemed restricted to small, profitable enterprises such as textile factories. There have been renewed efforts to expand the private sector by transferring ownership of large, strategic companies, and activity has increased, particularly involving foreign interests.

Finance

The Banque Central de Tunisie is the country's central bank and issues the dinar, the national currency. The government also partly operates several development banks, the largest of which is the Société Tunisienne de Banque, and there are numerous commercial banks. The dinar has been made partially convertible against the European Union (EU) euro and several other currencies. The Tunisian stock exchange, Bourse de Tunis, was founded in 1969 and has become a central pillar of economic policy, as it has facilitated privatization and encouraged both domestic savings and foreign investment.

Trade

Trade accounts for some one-fourth of GDP, and Tunisia relies heavily on its trade with Europe, with the EU accounting for the bulk of both exports and imports. France is the most important trading partner, followed by Italy, Germany, and China. Tunisia often shows an annual trade deficit. In the late 1990s the country signed an agreement with the EU, under the framework of the Euro-Mediterranean Partnership Program, that set in motion the creation of a free-trade area between Tunisia and the EU. Tunisia became a member of the General Agreement on Tariffs and Trade in 1990 and joined the World Trade Organization upon its founding in 1995. The country is also a signatory of the Arab League's Arab Free Trade Area. In addition, Tunisia is a member of the Arab

Maghrib Union, which aims at economic integration among its member states.

Tunisia's most significant exports are textiles and leather products, electrical machinery, and crude and refined petroleum. Its major imports are consumer products, raw materials, machinery and electrical equipment, and food products.

Services

Services, including retail trade, public administration, defense, and tourism, account for a significant portion of GDP although Tunisia's military spending, as a percentage of gross national product, is well below the world average and for nearly half of employment. Tourism has become one of Tunisia's leading sources of foreign exchange and has spawned a vibrant and growing handicraft industry in its wake. Although tourism was adversely affected by regional instabilities at the beginning of the 21st century, since the uprising against the regime of Zine al-Abidine Ben Ali in 2011, the number of tourists especially from other Arab countries has again been rising.

Labour and taxation

Unemployment in Tunisia has often been high, despite concerted efforts by the government to reduce the rate. Workers are allowed by law to organize, and there are a number of unions. The three large professional organizations are: the General Union of Tunisian Workers, the principal trade union; the Tunisian Union of Industry, Commerce and Handicrafts, the main employers' organization; and the National Union of Tunisian Farmers, the principal agricultural union. These are the main participants in national wage negotiations, although numerous other organizations also represent the country's economic interests.

Most government revenues are acquired through taxation, and Tunisia levies both direct and indirect taxes. Direct taxes take the form of an income tax assessed at a marginal rate and a flat-rate corporate tax. Indirect taxes include a variable-rate value-added tax(certain luxury items, for instance, are taxed at a higher rate) and professional training, social security, and registration taxes.

Transportation and telecommunications

The network of roads and railways is sufficiently dense so that all cities of any importance are linked with the interior. Nearly four-fifths of roads are paved. Tunisia is connected by both road and rail to Algeria but only by road to Libya, since the railway ends at Gabès. Work is under way to modernize and extend the railway network. The principal port is Tunis–La Goulette (Ḥalq al-Wādī); other major ports include Sfax, Bizerte, Sousse, and, in the south, Gabès. An oil pipeline runs from

Edjeleh, Algeria, to the port of La Skhira (Al-Ṣukhayrah) on the Gulf of Gabes.

Despite the construction of an airport at Gafsa, regional airports at Monastir (Al-Munastīr), Jerba (Jarbah), Sfax, and Tozeur handle domestic or charter flights, and international air traffic is directed mainly through Tunis-Carthage International Airport.

Tunisia's telecommunication services are controlled by Tunisie Télécom (founded in 1996), a state-owned entity that is responsible for maintaining and developing the country's communications infrastructure. Tunisia signed the World Trade Organization Basic Telecommunications Services Agreement of 1997, which opened the country's market, and its telecommunications infrastructure has expanded markedly since that time. Internet access is widespread, and cellular telephones far outnumber standard phone lines. Local communications are largely conducted over microwave radio links, while international transmission makes use of satellite networks and fibre-optic cables.

Government and Society

For nearly the entire period between Tunisia's achievement of independence in 1956 and the Jasmine Revolution, a popular uprising that unseated Pres. Zine al-Abidine Ben Ali in 2011, the Tunisian political system featured a powerful presidential regime backed by a single political party. The constitution of 1959 granted the president sweeping executive and legislative powers while placing narrow limits on the authority of the elected legislature and the judiciary. The Neo-Destour Party, led by Tunisia's first president, Habib Bourguiba, remained the only legal political party until 1981.

Some new political parties were permitted in 1981, permission for a multiparty system was granted in 1988, and the first multiparty elections were held in 1989. However, since the new political parties had neither the financial nor the organizational structure to mobilize serious opposition, Neo-Destour in 1988 renamed the Democratic Constitutional Rally and known by its French acronym, RCD retained a monopoly over political activity. Laws forbidding political parties based on ethnicity, religion, region, or language prevented the major opposition group, the Islamist Nahḍah ("Renaissance") Party, from being granted legal status, and many of its leaders were jailed or exiled. The exclusion of Islamists from politics came to an end in January 2011 with the downfall of the Ben Ali regime, and by late 2011 the Nahḍah

Party had emerged as the strongest party in the country, winning 90 seats in the 217 member Constituent Assembly tasked with drafting a new constitution to replace the suspended 1959 text.

Tensions between Islamists and liberals at times appeared to threaten Tunisia's transition to democracy, but, after more than two years of contentious negotiations, in January 2014 the Constituent Assembly voted overwhelmingly to approve a constitution that seemed to be acceptable to all sides. A caretaker government remained in power until legislative and presidential elections could be held.

Constitutional framework

The constitution proclaims Tunisia a republic with Arabic as its language and Islam as its religion. Freedom of expression and the right to form political parties and associations are guaranteed, as is freedom of religious belief.

Legislative authority is held by a single chamber, the Assembly of the People's Representatives. Members serve five-year terms. Following legislative elections, the president appoints a member of the winning party or coalition to form a cabinet. If a cabinet cannot be formed within four months, the president may dissolve the assembly and call for new legislative elections.

The president acts as head of state and exercises executive authority along with the prime minister and cabinet. The president is directly elected for a five-year term and may be reelected only once. Candidates for president must be Muslim, at least 35 years old, and Tunisian citizens by birth. The president is the commander in chief of the armed forces and conducts foreign policy but cannot declare war or enter treaties without the approval of the Assembly of the People's Representatives. The Assembly of the People's Representatives can impeach the president with a two-thirds vote.

Local government

The country is divided into 24 administrative areas called *wilāyāt* (provinces; singular *wilāyah*), each of which is headed by a *wālī* (governor). Each province is designated by the name of its chief town and is in turn subdivided into numerous units called *muʿtamadiyyāt* (delegations), whose number varies according to province size. Delegations are administered by a *muʿtamad* and are in turn divided into more than2,000 districts called *minṭaqah turābiyyah*s. Tunisia is further divided into scores of municipalities and rural councils.

Justice

Tunisia's legal system is based on French civil law with some influence from a liberal interpretation of Islamic law (Sharīʿah). The independence and neutrality of the courts are guaranteed by the constitution. The judiciary is made up of the courts of first instance, appellate courts, and the Court of Cassation. A separate system of administrative courts deals with legal disputes between individuals and state or public institutions, and cases concerning the management of public funds are handled by the Court of Audit. The Supreme Judicial Council, a body comprising judges and other legal specialists, oversees the functioning of the justice system.

The Constitutional Court rules on the constitutionality of laws and treaties. The court has 12 members, of whom four each are appointed by the president, Supreme Judicial Council, and

Assembly of the People's Representatives. Members serve a single nine-year term.

Political process

Since the Jasmine Revolution and the dissolution of the RCD in 2011, dozens of new political parties have gained formal recognition. The Nahḍah Party emerged as the strongest, and several centre-left parties also have significant support.

Since independence, a prominent feature of Tunisian social policy has been the effort to improve the status and lives of women. Compared with their counterparts in other Arabcountries, women in Tunisia have enjoyed greater equality before the law. The progressive Code of Personal Status, which was introduced in 1956, has been amended to affirm and enhance women's political, social, and economic roles. The constitution adopted in 2014 guarantees the equality of men and women before the law.

Security

Tunisia maintains a relatively small active-duty military, consisting mostly of conscripts whose term of service is one year. The army is the largest branch (with the highest number of conscripts), but the country also has a small navy and air force. The former consists mainly of small patrol vessels. The air force has relatively few high-performance aircraft. A national police force whose jurisdiction is largely restricted to the cities and a largely rural national guard report to the Ministry of the Interior and are responsible for national security.

Health and welfare

The living standards of the population in general are modest. The country's national health system provides nearly all of its population with access to medical care. Despite rising public expenditure on health, many Tunisians have been turning to private health care as demand outstrips supply. A good network of hospitals and clinics has contributed to a relatively low death rate and, in particular, to one of the lowest infant mortality rates on the African continent.

Housing

Traditional urban housing in Tunisia found in the old city centres, or medinas consisted of tightly arranged structures grouped within town walls and interlaced by a network of narrow walkways and passages. Building exteriors generally were whitewashed, with little decoration, while interiors were ornate and comfortable. Each neighbourhood (Arabic: *ḥārah*) was restricted to a particular ethnic or religious group, and it was only with the beginning of the protectorate that these city centres began to give way to European-style city plans. Following independence, the government began to encourage the restoration of the medinas, and architects have more recently sought to mitigate Western influence in favour of traditional architectural patterns.

Unique to the region are the underground dwellings found in the rural southeastern part of the country. These structures were designed for habitation in a harsh, arid environment and generally consist of a sunken central courtyard surrounded by individual family dwellings, storage areas, and workrooms, all of which are built into the earth. (Scenes from the motion picture *Star Wars* were filmed at such a dwelling located in the village of Matmata [Maṭmāṭah].)

Education

Education is free to all school-age children, and schooling is compulsory between the ages of 6 and

16. Virtually all of the country's children are enrolled in primary education, and nearly one-sixth of its young people go on to attend one of the country's universities or institutes of higher learning. More than three-fourths of the population is literate; the rate among men is somewhat higher than that among women, but the gap is narrowing.

Growth in the number of schools, students, and teachers has created a serious financial strain, as education has constituted one of the largest shares of the annual national budget. Students have had no alternative other than turning to private funding to supplement state education allowances, and they increasingly have been denied the choice of subject area or school. Given the difficulties of finding enough job opportunities for qualified people, more emphasis has been placed on technical, vocational, teacher, and agricultural training. The University of Tunis (founded 1960) is the country's major institution of higher education. Several more universities have opened since the 1980s, and there are also religious schools.

Cultural Life

Tunisians are an independent-minded people who take pride in the rich admixture of native and foreign influences that make up their national character. Their Arab-Muslim country was deeply imbued with French culture during the 75 years of the protectorate, which ended in 1956.

Daily life and social customs

In general, though Tunisians consider themselves to be more liberal and tolerant than their neighbours most urban women, for example, dress in Western clothes and do not veil themselves, and (though it is considered inappropriate by some Tunisian Muslims) locally made wines and spirits are consumed they still maintain a strong Islamic identity. Thus, Tunisians absorb new cultural influences from abroad while insisting on upholding their own values, but they are also vigilant about the impact of Western influence on their way of life. Those concerns led to a revival of some forms of social and religious conservatism in the 1990s, notably affecting women in the public sphere. Street cafés have increasingly become the preserve of men, especially in rural areas where relations between the sexes are still governed by conservative social norms.

Even Westernized Tunisians adhere to certain traditional values; foremost among these is the role of the family as the centre of social life. Meals are an important time for families to gather. Tunisian cuisine consists of a medley of European cuisine largely French and Italian and traditional dishes. As in the rest of the Maghrib, couscous, a semolina-based pasta, is a staple of virtually every meal and is customarily served with a rich stew. Other native basics are lamb, peppers, onions, chickpeas (often served in cakes as a dessert), and olive oil. Various types of seafood can be found near the coast. Unlike other cuisines of the Maghrib, Tunisian food is replete with hot spices, and *harissa*, a fiery red sauce, is served with most dishes.

Tunisians observe the standard Islamic holidays as well as several secular and national holidays, such as Independence Day (March 20) and Women's Day (August 13).

The arts

Dotted with the ruins of ancient civilizations, Tunisia is an important location for the study of world archaeology and architecture. Among the most significant of its numerous historic sites are

Al-Zaytūnah Mosque in Tunis, which dates to the 8th century CE, the slightly older Great Mosque of ʿUqbah ibn Nāfiʿ in Kairouan, and the remains of the ancient city of Carthage.

Although Tunisians generally use French or English in the scientific disciplines, they remain genuinely attached to Arabic in the literary sphere in poetry, the novel, and the short story. Historical figures of philosophy and literature, such as the 11th-century litterateurs Ibrāhīm al-Ḥuṣrī, Ḥasan ibn Rashīq, and Muḥammad ibn Sharaf al-Qayrawānī and the 14th-century polymath Ibn Khaldūn, are still revered. Modern Tunisian literature grew from a cultural renaissance in the early 20th century. Social essayist Tahar Haddad, satirist Ali Douagi, poet Aboul Kacem Chabbi, and others have paved the way for a new realist trend in Tunisian literature by combining modern European styles with contemporary Tunisian themes. Increasingly,

Tunisian writers, including women, are gaining international prominence.

Tunisian cinema has been gradually making its way to an international audience among the luminaries of the Tunisian cinema are the directors Moufida Tlatli (*Ṣamt al-Quṣūr* [1994; *The Silence of the Palaces*]) and Férid Boughedir (*Un été à La Goulette* [1995; *A Summer in La Goulette*]) and Tunisia has been the location for major motion pictureproductions, including *Star Wars* (1977) and *The English Patient* (1996).

Cultural institutions

Contemporary Tunisian painting can also lay claim to a certain tradition, with the École de Tunis being foremost among artistic institutions. Tunisian artists such as Hamadi Ben Saad and Hassen Soufy enjoy a genuine local celebrity and have also exhibited abroad. Musicand theatre-based cultural festivals notably the Carthage International Festival, the Testour Maalouf Festival of traditional Andalusian *malouf* (*maʾlūf*) music, the SousseInternational Cultural Festival, and the International Jazz Festival of Tabarka have become a feature of Tunisian life. Since Tunisians have generally been concerned about the influence of tourism on their social and cultural lives, the country's premier music conservatory, the Rashīdiyya Institute (1934), devotes attention mainly to national traditions while emphasizing classical European heritage. Tunisians are especially proud of El-Azifet, an exclusively female ensemble inspired by traditional *malouf* and *mouachah* (*muwashshaḥ*) music and traditional musicians such as Anouar Brahem.

The National Archives (1874) and the National Library (1885), both located in Tunis, contain large collections of documents, including books and manuscripts, the latter in Arabic and Ottoman Turkish. There are also a number of museums located throughout the country, the most notable of which is probably the Bardo National Museum (1888). This institution, located in the former palace of the Ottoman bey in the medina, or old quarter, of Tunis, houses collections of fine works dating from the Carthaginian, Roman, and Islamic periods. Among its holdings is the largest and possibly the finest collection of Roman mosaics in the world. The Carthage Museum (1964), a repository of numerous antiquities from the ancient and medieval periods, is located near the site of the ancient city and in close proximity to several important excavations. Several of these culturally significant locations in Tunisia have been designated UNESCO World Heritage sites, including Carthage and the medina of Tunis in 1979 and the historic city of Kairouan and the medina of Sousse in 1988.

Sports and recreation

Football (soccer) is the most popular modern sport. Tunisia has fielded teams for the African Cup of Nations and World Cup competitions. Football is also a family sport and has been important in creating a demand for satellite television. Athletics has also become popular in the country, and Tunisian runners have achieved international renown at middleand long-distance events. Tourism has provided resources for the development of other sports, including golf, hiking, and windsurfing. Scuba diving has benefited from a vigorous conservation program designed to protect the undersea flora and fauna. Tunisian women have not been excluded from participating in sports as women often have in other Arab countries and they have been encouraged to begin competing at an early age. The traditional sport of wild boar hunting is practiced mostly in the dunes, hills, and mountains of the Tabarka region.

Media and publishing

Until 2011 the Tunisian media operated under narrow constraints. Official censorship was augmented by self-censorship as various types of indirect government coercion restricted the ability of journalists and political personalities to speak freely. Nonetheless, the high rate of literacy and the sizable middle class helped to sustain an avid readership for the large number of periodicals (notably business and economics) published in Tunisia. The number of citizens with access to satellite television and the Internet has grown considerably since the late 1990s, although the government under Zine al-Abidine Ben Aliimposed what were believed to be among the world's tightest restrictions on Internet use.

The removal of the Ben Ali regime in January 2011 brought about sweeping changes. A number of private media outlets representing a variety of political viewpoints appeared, and the state-run Etablissement de la Radiodiffusion Télévision Tunisienne (ERTT) began to include open political debate in its television and radio programming.

The majority of the country's daily newspapers are in French, and French-language television and radio programs are broadcast daily along with those in Arabic and Italian.

The History

The following discussion offers a brief summary of Tunisia's early history but mainly focuses on Tunisia since about 1800. For a more detailed treatment of earlier periods and of the country in its regional context, *see* North Africa.

Tunisia was called Ifrīqiyyah in the early centuries of the Islamic period. That name, in turn, comes from the Roman word for Africa and the name also given by the Romans to their first African colony following the Punic Wars against the Carthaginians in 264–146 BCE. Following the decline of Rome, the region was ruled briefly by the Vandals and then the Byzantine Empire before being conquered by the Arabs in 647 CE. Although the Arabs initially unified North Africa, by 1230 a separate Tunisian dynasty had been established by the Ḥafṣids. Muslim Andalusians migrated to the area after having been forced out of Spain during the Reconquista, particularly following the defeat of the Muslim kingdom of Granada in 1492. By 1574, Tunisia was incorporated into the Ottoman Empire, whose control of the region, always tenuous, had all but dissolved by the 19th century.

Tunisia is the smallest of the Maghrib states and consequently the most cohesive. By the beginning of the 19th century, virtually all of its inhabitants spoke Arabic. Berber, the earlier language of the Maghrib, survived in Tunisia in only a few pockets, mainly in the extreme south. The vast majority of the population was Muslim, with a small Jewish minority. A single major city, Tunis, dominated the countryside both politically and culturally. Tunis itself was located near the site of the ancient city-state of Carthage. More easily controlled from within than any other Maghrib country, Tunisia was also more open to the influence of people and ideas from abroad. Roman Africa, for example, was the most intensively Christianized portion of North Africa, and Ifrīqiyyah was later more quickly and more thoroughly Islamicized.

A small state with limited resources, Tunisia nonetheless managed to retain considerable autonomy within the framework of the larger empires that frequently ruled it from afar. This status was achieved, for example, under the ʿAbbāsids in the 9th century and later under the Ottomans. Tunisia's geographic and historical legacy helped prepare it for the shocks it received in the 19th century as a land caught between an expanding Europe and a declining Ottoman Empire. Yet, Tunisia proved to be as vulnerable economically as it was militarily.

The growth of European influence

In 1830, at the time of the French invasion of Algiers, Tunisia was officially a province of the Ottoman Empire but in reality was an autonomous state. Because the principal military threat had long come from neighbouring Algeria, the reigning bey of Tunisia, Ḥusayn, cautiously went along with assurances from the French that they had no intention of colonizing Tunisia. Ḥusayn Bey even accepted the idea that Tunisian princes would rule the cities of Constantine and Oran. The scheme, however, had no chance of success and was soon abandoned.

Tunisia's security was directly threatened in 1835, when the Ottoman Empire deposed the ruling dynasty in Libya and reestablished direct Ottoman rule. Thereafter, the vulnerable *beylik* of Tunis found itself surrounded by two larger powers France and the Ottoman Empire both of which had designs on Tunisia. From that time until the establishment of the French protectorate in 1881, Tunisian rulers had to placate the larger powers while working to strengthen the state from within.

Aḥmad Bey, who ruled from 1837 to 1855, was an avowed modernizer and reformer. With the help of Western advisers (mainly French), he created a modern army and navy and related industries.

Conscription was also introduced, to the great dismay of the peasantry. More acceptable were Aḥmad's steps to integrate Arabic-speaking native Tunisians fully into the government, which had long been dominated by *mamlūk*s (military slaves) and Turks. Aḥmad abolished slavery and took other modernizing steps intended to bring Tunisia more in line with Europe, but he also exposed his country to Europe's infinitely greater economic and political power. His reforms negatively affected the already stagnant economy, which led to greater debt, higher taxes, and increased unrest in the countryside.

The next bey, Muḥammad (1855–59), tried to ignore Europe, but this was no longer possible. Continued civil disturbances and corruption prompted the British and French to force the bey to issue the Fundamental Pact (ʿAhd al-Amān;

September 1857), a civil rights charter modeled on the Ottoman rescript of 1839.

The final collapse of the Tunisian *beylik* came during the reign of Muḥammad al-Ṣādiq (1859–82). Though sympathetic to the need for reforms, Muḥammad was too weak either to control his own government or to keep the European powers at bay. He did, in 1861, proclaim the first constitution (*dustūr*; also *destour*) in the Arabic-speaking world, but this step toward representative government was cut short by runaway debt, a problem exacerbated by the government's practice of securing loans from European bankers at exorbitant rates.

When the principal minister, Muṣṭafā Khaznadār (who had served from the earliest days of Aḥmad Bey's reign), attempted to squeeze more taxes out of the hard-pressed peasants, the countryside rose in a revolt (1864). This uprising almost overthrew the regime, but the government ultimately suppressed it through a combination of guile and brutality.

Though Tunisia went bankrupt in 1869 and an international financial commission with British, French, and Italian representatives was imposed on the country, there was one last attempt to reform Tunisia from within and thus avoid complete European domination. It was made during the reformist ministry of Khayr al-Dīn (1873–77), one of the most effective statesmen of the 19th-century Muslim world. However, enemies from within and European intrigues from without conspired to force him from office. The final blow to Tunisia's sovereignty came at the Congress of Berlin in 1878, when Britainacquiesced to France's control of Tunisia.

On the pretext that Tunisians had encroached on Algerian territory, France invaded Tunisia in 1881 and imposed the Treaty of Bardo, which sanctioned French military occupation of Tunisia, transferred to France the bey's authority over finance and foreign relations, and provided for the appointment of a French resident minister as intermediary in all matters of common interest. This provoked an uprising in southern Tunisia during which France attacked and captured Sousse in July 1881, took Kairouan in October, and seized Gafsa and Gabès in November. After the death of Muḥammad al-Ṣādiq, his successor, ʿAlī, was forced to introduce administrative, judicial, and financial reforms that the French government considered useful. This agreement, known as the Convention of Al-Marsa, was signed in 1883 and solidified French control over Tunisia.

The protectorate (1881–1956)

Tunisia became a protectorate of France by treaty rather than by outright conquest, as was the case in Algeria. Officially, the bey remained an absolute monarch: Tunisian ministers were still appointed, the government structure was preserved, and Tunisians continued to be subjects of the bey. The French did not confiscate land, convert mosques into churches, or change the official language. Nevertheless, supreme authority was passed to the French resident general.

Under French guidance, Tunisia's finances were soon stabilized and modern communications established. Though France never overtly seized land or displaced the population, both of which had occurred in Algeria, the most fertile portions of northern Tunisia, comprising the Majardah valley and the Sharīk Peninsula, were passed on to other European countries. Valuable phosphate mines began operating near Gafsa in the south, and vegetables were cultivated and exported from the Majardah valley after French and Italian colonists had become established there.

By the 1890s a small French-educated group the members of which came to be called "Young Tunisians" began pushing for both modernizing reforms based on a European model and greater participation by Tunisians in their own government. The group's conduct during the protectorate, however, was cautious and reserved. Their major weapon became the newspaper *Le Tunisien*, a French-language publication founded in 1907. With the printing of an Arabic edition in 1909, the Young Tunisians simultaneously educated their compatriots and persuaded the more liberal French to help move Tunisia toward modernity.

Even this moderate protonationalism was subject to repressive measures by the French in 1911–12. Little nationalist activity took place during World War I (1914–18), but the first attempt at mass political organization came during the interwar period, when the Destour (Constitution) Party was created (the party was named for the short-lived Tunisian constitution of 1861). In 1920 the Destour Party presented the bey and the French government with a document that demanded that a constitutional form of government be established in which Tunisians would possess the same rights as Europeans. The immediate result was the arrest of ʿAbd al-ʿAzīz al-Thaʿālibī, the Destour leader. Two years later the aged bey, Muḥammad al-Nāṣir, requested that the program of the Destour be adopted or he would abdicate. In response, the resident general, Lucien Saint, surrounded the bey's palace with troops, and the demand was withdrawn. Saint thus introduced restrictive measures, together with minor reforms, that pacified Tunisian sentiment and weakened the nationalist movement for several years.

In 1934 a young Tunisian lawyer, Habib Bourguiba, and his colleagues broke with the Destour Party to form a new organization, the Neo-Destour, which aimed at spreading propaganda and gaining mass support. Under Bourguiba's vigorous leadership, the new party soon supplanted the existing Destour Party and its leaders. Attempts by the French to suppress the new movement only fueled the fire. The Neo-Destour began to gain more power and influence after the arrival of the Popular Front government in France in 1936. When the Popular Front government collapsed, repression was renewed in Tunisia and was met with civil disobedience. In 1938 serious disturbances led to the arrest of Bourguiba and other leaders of the party, which was then officially dissolved.

World War II

At the outbreak of war in 1939, Neo-Destour leaders, though still untried, were deported to France. However, they were released by the Nazis in 1942 following the German occupation of Vichy France, and, since Hitler regarded Tunisia as a sphere of Italian influence, he handed them over to the fascist government in Rome. There the leaders were treated with deference, the fascists hoping to gain support for the Axis. Bourguiba steadily refused to cooperate. In March 1943 he made a noncommittal broadcast, and the Neo-Destour leaders were finally allowed to proceed to Tunis, where the reigning bey, Muḥammad al-Munṣif (Moncef), formed a ministry of individuals who were sympathetic to Destour.

The assumption of power by the Free French after the Nazi retreat produced complete disillusionment for the Neo-Destour cause. The bey was deposed, while Bourguiba, accused of collaboration with the Nazis, escaped imprisonment by fleeing in disguise to Egypt in 1945. Still, a vigorous campaign of propaganda for Tunisian independence continued, and, in view of the emancipation of the eastern Arab states and later of neighbouring Libya, the French felt compelled to make concessions. In 1951 the French permitted a government with nationalist sympathies to take office of which the secretary-general of the Neo-Destour, Salah Ben Youssef, became a member and Bourguiba was allowed to return to Tunisia. When the newly formed government wished to establish a Tunisian parliament, however, further repressions ensued; Bourguiba was exiled, and most of the ministers were put under arrest. This resulted, for the first time, in outbreaks of terrorism. Nationalist guerrillas began to operate in the mountains, virtually paralyzing the country.

In July 1954 the French premier, Pierre Mendès-France, promised to grant complete autonomy to Tunisia, subject to a negotiated agreement. Bourguiba returned to Tunisia and was able to supervise the negotiations without directly participating. In June 1955 an agreement was finally signed by the Tunisian delegates though it imposed strict limits in the fields of foreign policy, education, defense, and finance and a mainly Neo-Destour ministry was formed. Salah Ben Youssef denounced the document, saying it was too restrictive, and refused to attend a specially summoned congress that unanimously supported Bourguiba. In response, he organized a brief armed resistance in the south that was quickly repressed.

Ben Youssef fled the country to escape imprisonment; he was assassinated in 1961.

Independence under the Neo-Destour Party (1956–2011)

The French granted full independence to Tunisia in an accord that was reached on March 20, 1956, and Bourguiba was chosen prime minister. The rule of the beys was subsequently abolished, and on July 25, 1957, a republic was declared, with Bourguiba as president.

Domestic development

After independence was granted, the Neo-Destour Party (from 1964 to 1988 the Destourian Socialist Party; from 1988 the Democratic Constitutional Rally [known by its French acronym RCD]) ensured that Tunisia moved quickly with reforms, most notably in the areas of education, the liberation of women, and legal reforms. Economic development was slower, but the government paid considerable attention to the more impoverished parts of the country. In 1961 Ahmad Ben Salah took charge of planning and finance. His ambitious efforts at forced-pace modernization, especially in agriculture, were foiled, however, by rural and conservative opposition. Expelled from the party and imprisoned in 1969, Ben Salah escaped in 1973 to live in exile. His fall brought a move in the government toward more conservative alignment.

In 1975 the Chamber of Deputies unanimously bestowed the presidency for life on the sick and aging Habib Bourguiba, who centralized power under his progressive but increasingly personalized rule. Hedi Amira Nouira, noted for his financial and administrative skills, became prime minister in November 1970, but his government failed to resolve the economic crisis or address growing demands for reform from liberals in his own party.

A decade later, the ailing Nouira was replaced by Muhammad Mzali, who made efforts to restore dissidents to the party and by 1981 had granted amnesty to many who had been jailed for earlier disturbances. In addition, he persuaded Bourguiba to accept a multiparty system (although only one opposition party was actually legalized).

The outcome of the elections in November 1981 was disappointing to those who sought political liberalization. The National Front, an alliance of the Destourian Socialist Party and the trade union movement, swept all 136 parliamentary seats, a result received with cynicism and dismay by the opposition. Meanwhile, an Islamist opposition was developing around the Islamic Tendency Movement (Mouvement de la Tendance Islamique [MTI]). By 1984 Bourguiba had perceived an Islamist hand behind riots and demonstrations protesting rising prices. In response, he sent in the army and initiated a fierce campaign against the MTI. Bourguiba's long rule, widely popular in its early years except among traditionalist groups, had provoked an increasing but passive opposition among Tunisians. Bourguiba, long in declining health, became unable to mask his autocratic tendencies. National elections in 1986 were boycotted by the major opposition parties, and the National Front once again carried the vote. In November 1987, amid widespread unrest and growing Islamist support, Bourguiba was declared mentally unfit to rule and was removed from office. He was succeeded by General Zine al-Abidine Ben Ali, whom he had appointed as prime minister a month earlier.

President Ben Ali promised political liberalization and a transition to democracy. His early reforms attempted to restore a national consensus; one of these, the National Pact signed in 1989, drew together the ruling party, the legal opposition, the Islamists, and all the national organizations. Many political parties were legalized, with the exception of the MTI (renamed the Nahḍah ["Renaissance"] Party in 1988), but the 1989 national elections still failed to introduce a multiparty competition. The president gained 99 percent of the vote, and the RCD won all 141 seats in the legislature. Local elections in 1990, boycotted by opposition parties, were also swept by the ruling party. Following early local electoral victories by Algerian Islamists in 1990 and Islamist opposition to the Persian Gulf War(1990–91), the government began to crack down on Islamist political activity.

Although the government initially eased press controls and released political prisoners, the opposition soon became disillusioned with the new regime. Subsequently the government turned against secular opposition, and it has since been criticized for its abuse of human rights and its reliance on military and security forces. Piecemeal electoral reforms have failed to produce any genuine form of power sharing or transfer of power away from the president or his party (Ben Ali won reelection in 1994, 1999, 2004, and 2009, each time by an overwhelming margin). Similarly, the media and national organizations and associations have lost much of what little autonomy they had wrested from the state, and Ben Ali's regime became increasingly subject to accusations of authoritarianism. The government, for its part, has claimed that democratization must be a gradual process that cannot be allowed to destabilize or inhibit the processes of economic liberalization and social consolidation. The implementation of a bicameral legislature in 2005 was given as a step toward political liberalization.

Foreign relations

Foreign relations under Habib Bourguiba were dominated by his personal conviction that Tunisia's future lay with the West and, in particular, with France and the United States. There were, nonetheless, some early crises, including a French bombing raid on the Tunisian village of Sakiet Sidi Youssef (Sāqiyat Sīdī Yūsuf) in 1958, during which France claimed the right to pursue Algerian rebels across the border; the Bizerte incident of 1961, concerning the continued military use of that port and airfield facility by France; and the suspension of all French aid in 1964–66 after Tunisia abruptly nationalized foreign-owned landholdings. These difficulties aside, Tunisia's relations with France have been improving, as have relations with the United States, despite some tensions with the latter over its involvement in the Persian Gulf War and its policies toward the developing world. Alignment with the West was never allowed to interfere with positive trade policies with developing countries and what was then the Soviet bloc. Rather than balance East against West, Bourguiba maximized Tunisia's advantages by maintaining good relations with both and thereby reduced the country's dependency on either one. Bourguiba's pragmatism also extended to the Arab world. Rejecting ideological constraints, he argued for the Arab recognition of Israel and Arab unity based on mutually advantageous cooperation rather than political integration.

Under Ben Ali, Tunisia followed much the same path. The need for regional security and the desire to advance economic interests, especially trade and foreign investment, guided foreign policy. With the uncertain future and stability of the Arab Maghrib Union, Tunisia increasingly concentrated efforts on developing bilateral economic agreements with other Arab states, on promoting the Arab League's Arab Free Trade Area, and in advancing regional economics. An agreement with the European Union, which came into effect in 1998, also tied Tunisia's economy and security to the Mediterranean community. Attempts to diversify trading links led to closer ties with the East and Southeast Asia, and strong ties with the United States remained a linchpin in Tunisia's ability to present itself as a stable, reliable, and moderate state. Tunisia has been keen on supporting international organizations, in particular the United Nations, which it has viewed as the protector of smaller states and the defender of international law.

The Jasmine Revolution

Ouster of Zine al-Abidine Ben Ali

In January 2011 Ben Ali was forced out of power by a popular uprising that came to be known as the Jasmine Revolution. The demonstrations, and Ben

Ali's ouster, inspired a series of uprisings known as the Arab Spring, especially in Egypt, Yemen, Libya, and Syria. Tunisia's revolution is widely considered to be the only one of these uprisings to have succeeded in replacing an autocratic government with a stable democratic government.

Unrest began after Mohammed Bouazizi, an unemployed 26-year-old, protested government corruption by setting fire to himself outside a municipal office in the town of Sidi Bouzid in central Tunisia on December 17, 2010. Bouazizi, who had been supporting his family by selling fruit from a cart, was enraged when local officials repeatedly demanded bribes and confiscated his merchandise. His plight, which came to symbolize the injustice and economic hardship afflicting many Tunisians under the Ben Ali regime, inspired street protests throughout the country against high unemployment, poverty, and political repression.

The Tunisian government's response to the protests attracted international criticismwhen dozens of protesters were killed in clashes with police. Amid accusations of use of excessive force, Ben Ali dismissed the minister of the interior, Rafik Belhaj Kacem, and vowed to establish an investigative committee to examine the government's response to the crisis. However, clashes between police and protesters continued and spread to the capital, where the government deployed troops to control the unrest. Because earlier attempts to quell the rioting had failed, on January 13 Ben Ali appeared on national television and made broader concessions to the opposition, promising not to seek another term as president when his term ends in 2014. He expressed regret over the deaths of protesters and vowed to order police to stop using live fire except in self-defense. Addressing some of the protesters' grievances, he said he would reduce food prices and loosen restrictions on Internet use. However, Ben Ali's concessions did not satisfy the protesters, who continued to clash with security forces, resulting in several deaths.

On January 14 a state of emergency was declared, and Tunisian state media reported that the government had been dissolved and that legislative elections would be held in the next six months. That announcement also failed to quell unrest, and Ben Ali stepped down as president, leaving the country. The prime minister, Mohamed Ghannouchi, assumed power. The following day Ghannouchi was replaced as interim president by Fouad Mebazaa, the former speaker of the lower house of the Tunisian parliament. Both were members of Ben Ali's political party, the RCD.

Transition

Disorder lingered in Tunisia in the days after Ben Ali's departure. Protests continued, with many objecting to the participation of RCD politicians in the interim government. There were also sporadic outbreaks of violence that many Tunisians attributed to Ben Ali loyalists attempting to sow chaos in the country.

On January 17 Ghannouchi, once again acting as prime minister, announced the formation of a new unity government that incorporated several opposition figures in cabinet posts alongside several sitting ministers from the Ben Ali regime. Ghannouchi defended the presence of ministers from the previous regime in the new government, saying that the ministers had not participated in Ben Ali's attempts to violently suppress protests. He also announced that the interim government would act quickly to preserve economic stability and to establish political freedom in Tunisia, releasing political prisoners and eliminating media censorship. The next day, however, the future of the interim government appeared to be in jeopardy when a number of the cabinet's new ministers from opposition parties resigned in response to fresh street protests over the inclusion of ministers from the previous regime. Attempting to signal a break with the past, Mebazaa, Ghannouchi, and the interim government's cabinet ministers who had served under Ben Ali all withdrew from the RCD. The interim government announced another set of reforms, lifting Ben Ali's ban on opposition political parties and granting amnesty to all political prisoners. However, demonstrators continued to hold rallies to protest the interim government's close ties to the Ben Ali regime. On February 6 the RCD was officially suspended, and on February 27 Ghannouchi stepped down as prime minister. He was replaced by Beji Caid Sebsi, who had served as foreign minister under Bourguiba.

On March 7 the interim government led by Sebsi acceded to one of the pro-democracy movement's principal demands by dissolving Tunisia's secret police force, which had played an important role in suppressing political dissent under the Ben Ali regime. The interim government issued a statement reaffirming its intention to respect Tunisians' rights and freedoms and rejecting the use of security forces for political purposes.

Tunisians voted on October 23, 2011, to determine the composition of the 217-member Constituent Assembly, a new body with a mandate to appoint an interim cabinet and draft a new constitution. With voter turnout at nearly 70 percent, the moderate Islamist Nahḍah Party emerged as the clear victor, winning 90 seats with more than 40 percent of the vote. The election, the first since the ouster of Ben Ali, was described by observers as free and fair. The Constituent Assembly met for the first time in late November and approved an interim constitution in early December. The assembly also elected Moncef Marzouki, a human rights activist and former opponent of the Ben Ali regime, as president of Tunisia. Marzouki then appointed Hamadi Jebali, a member of the Nahḍah Party, to the post of prime minister.

Factional tension, compromise, and a new constitution

After the removal of Ben Ali, whose regime had repressed any form of Islamist activity, the polarization between secular and religious factions became a dominant feature of Tunisian political life. The emergence of a hard-line Salafist movement placed pressure on the Islamist Nahḍah

Party, usually considered moderate and pragmatic, to guarantee a significant role for Islamic law in the new constitution.

The growing tension between secular and Islamist factions was accompanied by deterioration in public security in 2012 and early 2013. Secularists accused the Nahḍah Party government of giving tacit approval to a series of riots and other acts of violence by groups of Salafists, and their fears were heightened by the assassination of a leftist politician, Chokri Belaid, in February 2013. Although the identity of Belaid's killers remained unknown, the assassination touched off a political crisis. Secularists, increasingly convinced that they were the targets of an Islamist intimidation campaign, held mass demonstrations, and several members of the cabinet resigned their positions. The incident also brought down Jebali, who resigned as prime minister when the Nahḍah Party rejected his proposal to reduce tension by forming a new cabinet of technocrats. The assassination of a second secular opposition politician, Mohamed Brahimi, in July threatened to derail the drafting of a new constitution in the Constituent Assembly, but in October the Nahḍah Party eased tensions by agreeing to hand over power to a caretaker interim cabinet.

Negotiations over the drafting of a new constitution moved forward in late 2013 after Nahḍah Party leaders made a number of concessions to secularists and liberals regarding the status of Islam in public life. In January 2014 the Constituent Assembly completed and approved a constitution, 200 voting in favour and 12 against with 4 abstentions. The new document was praised by Tunisian leaders and international observers as an example of successful compromise between Islamist and secular parties.

Unity government

The swing away from Islamists continued in legislative and presidential elections, both held in late 2014. In October the secular Nida Tounes party, led by Sebsi, won 85 seats of the 217 in Tunisia's new legislative assembly, the Assembly of the Representatives of the People, while the Nahḍah Party won only 69. In December Sebsi himself was elected president, winning more that 55 percent of the vote in a runoff against the incumbent interim president, Marzouki. With no party in a position to form a parliamentary majority, Nida Tounes and the Nahḍah Party agreed to form a unity government. The two parties worked together to promote a stable government in order to effect economic recovery.

The road was rocky, however. Tunisia's tourism industry suffered a new blow when, in March 2015, gunmen from a group affiliated with the

Islamic State in Iraq and the Levant(ISIL; also called ISIS) stormed the National Bardo Museum in Tunis, killing 21 people, most of whom were foreign tourists. A second attack came in June when another gunman with links to ISIL shot tourists on a beach in the resort town of Sousse, killing 39. Moreover, unemployment remained high, and the government's inability to stabilize the economy and create jobs prompted renewed demonstrations.

In July 2016 the parliament dismissed the government of Prime Minister Habib Essid, and Youssef Chahed became Tunisia's seventh prime minister in five years. In late 2017, facing international pressure to reduce the trade deficit and attract international investment, the government enacted a number of austerity measures that included higher taxes and prices of basic goods. Protesters took to the streets once again in January 2018. Leaders of Nida Tounes began to call on Chahed to resign, while the Nahḍah Party continued to support him in effort to maintain a stable premiership. Some members of Nida Tounes also continued to support Chahed's premiership, and, in September eight parliament members of Nida Tounes left the party in order to prevent a vote of no confidence against Chahed.

The End

Made in United States
North Haven, CT
28 July 2022

21973426R00139